ADOBE
PHOTOSHOP 2024

For beginners and Advanced Users

Your Complete Guide to Mastering Illustration with New Features, Updated Tools, and Easy Shortcuts for Every Skill Level

Ryson Thalian

Disclaimer and Terms of Use

The author and publisher of this book and the accompanying materials have used their best efforts in preparing this book. The author and publisher make no representation or warranties concerning the accuracy, applicability, fitness, or completeness of the contents of this book. The information contained in this book is strictly for informational purposes.

Printed in the United States of America

TABLE OF CONTENTS

INTRODUCTION

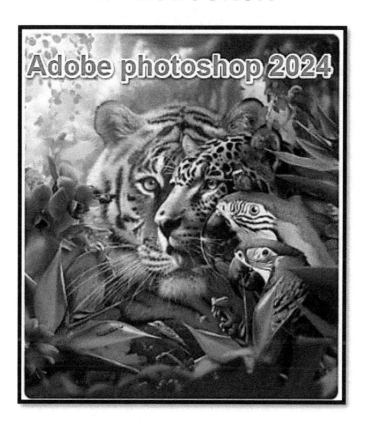

Step into the realm of Adobe Photoshop 2024! As we embark on this new decade, this iconic software remains a pioneering force in the realm of digital imaging and design. With its formidable toolkit and boundless potential, Photoshop stands as the ultimate choice for photographers, graphic designers, and artists. In this introduction, we will embark on a journey through the latest innovations and enhancements that Adobe has brought to Photoshop 2024, witnessing how it perpetually redefines the art of crafting and manipulating visual content. Join us as we delve into the ever-evolving landscape of this potent program, adapted to meet the dynamic demands of the digital era.

Adobe Photoshop continues to lead the way in this fast-paced age of technological innovation by constantly expanding the boundaries of creativity and providing users with powerful tools to make their ideas a reality. Whether you're an experienced graphic designer, a photography enthusiast, or just enjoy working with and improving images, this version of Photoshop offers a ton of exciting new features and enhancements that will help you become a better artist. Come along as we explore the limitless possibilities of Adobe Photoshop 2024 and how it can completely change the way that image creation and alteration are done.

Adobe Photoshop 2024 is the most recent iteration of the widely recognized image editing software globally. Renowned for its extensive support for a variety of creative tasks, from graphic design to photo retouching, and for its vast range of tools and outstanding editing skills.

There are a ton of new and intriguing features coming with Adobe Photoshop 2024, such as:

1. **Enhanced Performance**: Adobe has fine-tuned the program for optimized performance, ensuring smooth operation on Windows systems.
2. **Sky Replacement Tool**: This innovative feature simplifies the process of replacing and enhancing the sky in your photos, enabling the addition of dramatic effects to your images.
3. **Object Selection Tool**: The object selection tool has been refined, making it easier to select and manipulate specific elements within your images.
4. **Neural Filters**: Dive into the world of creative filters with Neural Filters, which harness AI technology to deliver stunning and unique results.

5. **Advanced Warping**: The new Warp mode offers precise image reshaping with enhanced flexibility and accuracy.

CHAPTER ONE

SYSTEM REQUIREMENT, DOWNLOADING AND INSTALLING PHOTOSHOP 2024

Minimum and Recommended System Requirements for Photoshop (Windows)

Here are the system requirements for Adobe Photoshop 2024 (Windows), including both minimum and recommended configurations:

Minimum System Requirements:

- Processor: Intel® or AMD processor with 64-bit support; 2 GHz or faster processor with SSE 4.2 or later.
- Operating System: Windows 10 64-bit (version 22H2) or later; LTSC versions are not supported.
- RAM: 8 GB.
- Graphics Card: 1.5 GB of GPU memory and support for DirectX 12.
- Monitor Resolution: 100% UI scaling on a 1280 x 800 monitor.
- Hard Drive Space: There is 20 GB of free hard drive space.
- Internet: To validate subscriptions, activate required software, and use online services, you must have an internet connection and register.

Recommended System Requirements:

- Processor: Intel® or AMD processor with 64-bit support; 2 GHz or faster processor with SSE 4.2 and AVX support.

- Operating System: Windows 10 64-bit (version 22H2) or later; LTSC versions are not supported.
- RAM: 16 GB or more.
- Graphics Card: GPU with DirectX 12 support and 4 GB of GPU memory for 4k displays and greater.
- Monitor Resolution: 1920 x 1080 display or greater at 100% UI scaling.
- Hard disk space: an independent internal drive for scratch drives and a 100 GB quick internal SSD for program installation.
- Internet: To validate subscriptions, activate required software, and use online services, you must have an internet connection and register.

Minimum and Recommended System Requirements for Photoshop (MacOS)

Here are the system requirements for Adobe Photoshop 2024 (macOS), including both minimum and recommended configurations:

Minimum System Requirements:

- CPU: 64-bit compatible multicore Intel® or Apple Silicon CPU with a speed of up to 2 GHz and SSE 4.2 or later.
- Operating System: 11.0 or later macOS Big Sur.

- RAM: 8 GB.
- Graphics Card: GPU with DirectX 12 support and 1.5 GB of GPU memory.
- Monitor Resolution: 1280 x 800 display at 100% UI scaling.
- Hard Disk Space: 20 GB of available hard disk space.

Recommended System Requirements:
- Processor: Apple Silicon, an ARM-based processor.
- MacOS Ventura (version 13.5.1) is the operating system.
- Memory: at least 16 GB.
- Graphics Card: 4 GB of GPU memory for 4K screens and support for DirectX 12.
- Monitor Resolution: 100% UI scaling at 1920 x 1080 pixels or higher on display.
- Hard Disk Space: There is 100 GB available. Two internal drives: one for scratch disks and one for quick internal SSD app installation.

Installing Adobe Photoshop 2024 (Version 25.0)

Downloading Adobe Photoshop 2024:

1. Visit the official Adobe website and navigate to the Photoshop product page.

2. Click on the install button.

3. Use your Adobe ID to log in. or create one if you don't have an account.

4. Choose your subscription plan and preferred payment method.

5. Once your purchase is complete, the download will commence automatically. After you have successfully purchased the license or provided information for the trial period, you will prompted to download the Adobe Creative installer.

6. Download and install the Creative Cloud app by following the on-screen instructions.

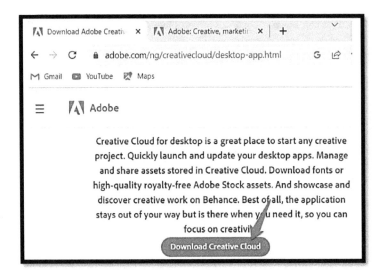

Installing Adobe Photoshop 2024:

1. After the installer is downloaded, run the setup file.
2. Follow the on-screen instructions, which may include selecting the installation location.
3. The installation process may take a few minutes.
4. Once the installation is finished, Adobe Photoshop 2024 is ready to use.

CHAPTER TWO

LAUNCHING PHOTOSHOP

Once you have installed Photoshop 2024, you can launch it in different ways depending on your operating system. For Windows users, you can launch it from the Start menu, the desktop shortcut, or the Adobe Creative Cloud app. For macOS users, you can launch it from the Applications folder or the Dock.

Adobe Photoshop 2024 is part of the Adobe Creative Cloud suite. To begin using Photoshop 2024, you must first install the desktop version of Creative Cloud. You can obtain the app from Adobe's official website or follow the link provided in your Creative Cloud subscription.

Step 1: Launch Adobe Photoshop 2024

After installing Creative Cloud, launch the application and use your Adobe ID to log in. and password. In the "Apps" tab, you'll find all the available Creative Cloud applications. Click on the "Photoshop 2024" icon to open the program.

Step 2: Sign In

Upon launching Photoshop 2024, you will be prompted to use your Adobe ID to log in and password. Enter your credentials and click "Sign In."

Step 3: Choose Your Workspace

When you initially open Photoshop 2024, you'll be asked to select a workspace. You can choose from "Photography," "Design," "3D," or "Motion." Each workspace is tailored to specific types of work, but you can change your workspace at any time by going to Window > Workspace.

Step 4: Make a New Document

Click "File" in the top menu bar and select "New" to start a new document. The keyboard shortcuts Ctrl+N for Windows and Command+N for Mac can also be used. This will launch the new document dialog box, where you may adjust the project's dimensions, resolution, and other parameters.

Step 5: Access a Current Document

To access an already-existing document click on "File" in the top menu bar and select "Open." Alternatively, you can use the shortcut Ctrl+O (Windows) or Command+O (Mac). This will open a file explorer window, allowing you to navigate to the location of your document and open it.

Step 6: Start Editing

Once you have opened a new or existing document, you can begin editing your picture with the various tools and features in Photoshop 2024. Access different tools and settings through the top menu bar, the left-hand toolbar, and the panels on the right.

Get Acquainted with the Home Screen

1. When you launch Adobe Photoshop 2024, the first screen you see is the home screen. You may access tutorials and sample files, create new projects, and retrieve current projects from this handy starting point.

2. There are three primary categories on the home screen: **Learn, Make New, and Recent.** Clicking the arrows next to each heading will collapse or enlarge each of these parts.

3. The projects that you have recently opened are shown in the recent section. You can open a project by clicking on it, or you can find the project on your computer quickly by using the Show in Explorer/Finder option.

4. In the Create New section, you can initiate a new project. This section offers a variety of project types, including photo editing, illustration, graphic design, and web design. Click on a project type to explore available templates or utilize the search field to locate a specific template.

5. The Learn section grants access to tutorials and sample files to enhance your Photoshop skills. You can explore various categories or utilize the search bar to find specific tutorials or sample files.

6. At the lower section of the home screen, you'll find options to access your Adobe account, access your cloud documents, or access a help center.

7. You can personalize the home screen by clicking the gear icon in the upper right corner. From there, you can adjust settings, including background color, section display preferences, and other configurations.

8. All you have to do is click the "Open a document" button located at the screen's bottom to jump straight to the Photoshop workspace and leave the home screen behind.

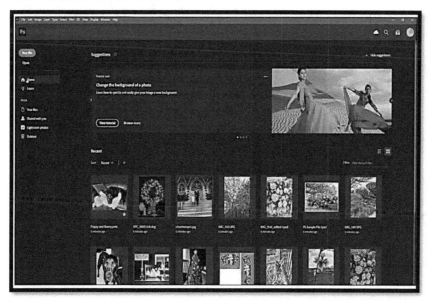

Familiarizing with the Photoshop Workspace

1. **Launch Adobe Photoshop 2024**: Begin by opening Adobe Photoshop 2024 on your computer.

2. **Navigate the Menu Bar**: The Menu Bar sits at the top of the Photoshop window and houses essential options and commands for image editing, including File, Edit, Layer, Image, Filter, View, Window, and Help are among the options. Take some time to familiarize yourself with these options and their respective functions.

3. **Discover the Tools Panel**: The Tools panel is typically located on the left side of the Photoshop window and offers a variety of tools for image creation, selection, and editing. Hover your cursor over each tool to identify its name and purpose.

4. **Utilize the Panels:** Panels are situated on the right side of the Photoshop workspace and contain specific options and settings for

various tasks. By default, you'll have access to the Layers, Properties, and History panels. To open additional panels, navigate to the Window menu and select your desired panel.

5. **Understand the Options Bar**: The Options bar, located just beneath the Menu Bar, adjusts based on the selected tool, displaying relevant options and settings for that tool. To become acquainted use the Options bar, select different tools, and observe how the options change accordingly.

6. **Personalize Your Workspace**: Tailor your workspace to your preferences by rearranging and resizing panels, tools, and options. You can even save a custom workspace for different project types.

7. **Experiment with Fundamental Functions**: To become comfortable with the Photoshop workspace, engage in practical exercises involving essential functions. These may include generating a fresh document, opening existing images, utilizing various tools, and adjusting panel options. Such experimentation enhances your understanding of how the various workspace elements interact.

When you choose and access a cloud document, you step into the editing environment, where you'll discover a host of familiar Photoshop tools, panels, and various features. These resources enable you to efficiently craft stunning compositions and make swift creative touch-ups while you're on the move. The canvas, the space where you directly interact with your open document, forms the central focus of your creative endeavors.

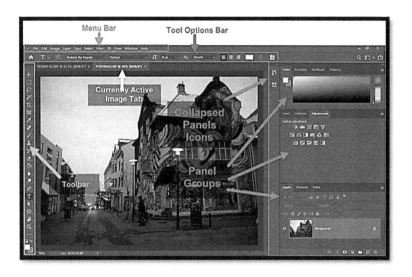

Exploring the Toolbar

The toolbar in Adobe Photoshop 2024 is a pivotal and frequently utilized element, housing a diverse array of tools designed for image editing, creation, and manipulation. Let's delve into some of the primary tools and their respective functions.

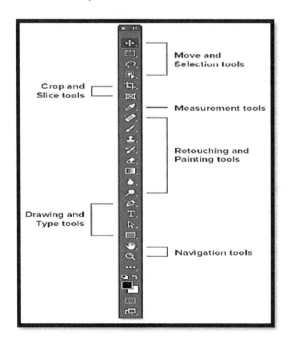

Selection Tools Group

The "Selection Tools" group in Adobe Photoshop 2024 comprises a set of tools designed for precisely selecting specific portions of an image or graphic. These tools are fundamental for image editing, retouching, and manipulation within Photoshop. Below are the selection tools that constitute this group:

1. **Marquee Tool:** With this tool, you can create selections in rectangular, elliptical, or single row/column shapes.
2. **Lasso Tool:** The Lasso Tool empowers you to make freehand selections by manually drawing selection outlines.

3. **Quick Selection Tool:** This tool assists in creating selections based on similar colors and textures found in an image.
4. **Magic Wand Tool:** It selects pixels within an image based on color similarity, simplifying the selection process.
5. **Crop Tool:** Use this tool to crop or eliminate unwanted portions of an image.
6. **Slice Tool:** For web optimization, this tool facilitates the creation and editing of image slices.
7. **Perspective Crop Tool:** It enables you to resize a picture while adjusting its perspective.
8. **Slice Select Tool:** This tool is employed to choose and modify individual slices in an image.
9. **Content-Aware Move Tool:** With this tool, you can move and extend objects within an image while the background is automatically filled in.
10. **Selection Brush Tool:** To make precise selections, you can use this tool to paint over the desired area.

11.**Quick Mask Tool:** The Quick Mask Tool lets you create temporary selections by applying a red overlay.

12.**Refine Edge Brush Tool:** It is very beneficial for fine-tuning the edges of selections, especially when working with intricate subjects like hair or fur.

13.**Color Range Tool:** This tool selects specific colors within an image, offering precise control over your selections.

14.**Focus Area Tool:** The Focus Area Tool automatically selects the in-focus areas of an image.

15.**Select and Mask Workspace:** This workspace provides an array of tools and options for enhancing and altering selections, ensuring your edits are refined to perfection.

Group of Crop and Slice Tools

The "Slice and Crop Implements in Adobe Photoshop 2024 encompasses an array of tools dedicated to cropping and slicing images. These tools are invaluable for selectively removing portions of an image or dividing it into segments. Below are the tools and options found in this group.

1. **Crop Tool:** Used to resize and trim an image by adjusting the handles on its corners or specifying precise dimensions.

2. **Perspective Crop Tool:** This allows you to modify an image's perspective while cropping it.

3. **Slice Tool:** Partitions a picture into multiple sections, aiding in web optimization.

4. **Slice Select Tool:** Permits the selection and manipulation of individual slices within an image.

5. **Slice Tool Options:** Customizable settings for creating and modifying slices.

6. **Options for Slice Select Tool:** Adjustable settings for selecting and modifying slices.

7. **Content-Aware Crop Tool:** Utilizes content-aware technology to automatically fill in gaps when reducing the size of an image.

8. **Trim Tool:** Enables the trimming of transparent areas around an image.

9. **Perspective Warp:** Adjusts the perspective of specific areas within an image.

10. **Perspective Grid Tool:** Adds a grid to an image, aiding in aligning objects with a specific perspective.

11. **Vanishing Point:** Helps define perspective planes and seamlessly move objects between them.

12. **Ruler Tool:** Measures distances within an image.

13. **Count Tool:** Useful for counting objects within an image.

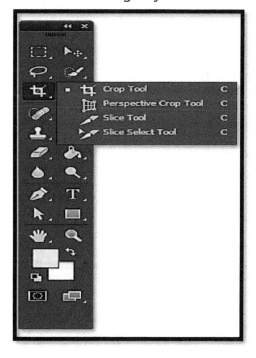

Measuring Tools Group

The "Measuring Tools" group is a set of tools designed to enable users to make accurate measurements and alignments within their images. These tools are especially valuable for professionals like designers and architects who require precise measurements in their work.

1. **Ruler Tool:** The primary tool in this group, the Ruler tool, empowers users to draw straight lines and measure distances in their images. It can be accessed by clicking and dragging from the upper or left ruler of the canvas or by selecting it from the Tools panel. This tool provides options to modify the unit of measurement and constrain lines to specific angles.

2. **Protractor Tool:** Similar to the Ruler tool, the Protractor tool can measure both angles and distances. Users can access it by clicking and dragging the protractor icon from the Tools panel.

3. **Count Tool:** The Count tool is ideal for tallying pixels or objects within a selected area, making it invaluable for determining the size of elements in a picture or creating pixel-perfect designs.

4. **Eyedropper Tool:** Although not primarily a measuring tool, The Eyedropper instrument can be used for precise color measurements. Users can drag and click with this tool to obtain the exact color values of a pixel, including RGB, CMYK, and hexadecimal values, within their image.

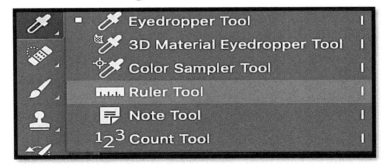

Type Tools Group

The type Tools Group" is a comprehensive set of tools made especially for using the program to create, edit, and format text. With the aid of these tools, users can add text, create complex text effects, and alter text in several ways.

Key tools within this group include:

1. **Horizontal Type Tool**: This is the standard instrument for creating horizontally oriented text.
2. **Vertical Type Tool**: Used for vertically oriented text.
3. **Tool for Vertical Type Masking:** Allows the creation of a mask that can be filled with vertical text.
4. **Type Mask Tool**: This tool enables users to create a text selection on an image, which can then be filled with color or an image.
5. **Use a Path Tool to Type:** Permits the creation of text next to a path, such as a curve or shape.
6. **Warp Text Tool**: Empowers users to manipulate the shape of text, resulting in effects like arching or bulging.

Within the Type Tools Group, you'll find various formatting options, including text alignment, font selection, font size, and more. Users can also apply effects to text, such as drop shadows, outlines, and bevels.

A noteworthy addition to the Type Tools Group in Adobe Photoshop 2024 is the "Smart Type Layer" option. This feature automatically resizes text to fit within a designated area, simplifying the process of creating professional-looking designs with consistent text sizes.

Overall, the Type Tools Group offers a comprehensive array of tools for working with text in diverse ways. Designers can enjoy greater control and flexibility when handling text, making it easy to add text to their designs and experiment with various effects and styles.

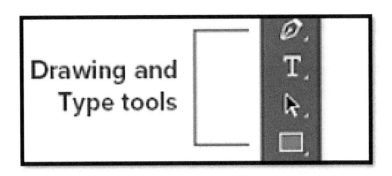

Navigation Tools Group

The group of tools called the "Navigation Tools Group" are intended to make navigating and viewing images easier. With the help of these tools, users may navigate around the canvas with ease, enlarge and reduce photos with efficiency, and identify specific locations within them.

The tools encompassed in the Navigation Tools Group are as follows:

1. **Hand Tool**. This tool empowers users to navigate the canvas by clicking and dragging, making it especially valuable when working on expansive images and switching between different regions.
2. **Zoom Tool**: Users can use the Zoom tool to magnify or reduce the image size. They can either use the "+" and "-" keys for gradual adjustments or the scrubby zoom feature for rapid zoom level changes.
3. **Zoom Out Tool**: For a swift, single-click zoom-out, this tool proves convenient, providing an immediate overview of the entire image.
4. **Navigator Panel**: This panel offers a visual depiction of the image, with a red rectangle indicating the presently visible area. Users can click and drag this rectangle to traverse the canvas.

5. **Hand/Zoom Options**: These options extend settings for the Hand and Zoom tools, such as zooming using the mouse scroll wheel or entering a specific zoom percentage.

6. **Pan Behind Tool**: When users need to move the view's center without impacting the image's layers or objects, this tool is invaluable. It is beneficial for aligning elements or adjusting perspectives.

Retouching Tools Group

The "Retouching Tools Group" includes an essential set of tools designed for picture manipulation and improvement. These tools are essential for helping photographers and artists produce work that is polished and looks professional. We examine the several instruments in this category and their corresponding uses below:

1. **Healing Spot Brush Instrument**
   - Purpose: Ideal for addressing minor imperfections and blemishes in an image.
   - Function: Automatically samples surrounding pixels and seamlessly blends them with the area being edited.

2. **Healing Brush Tool**
   - Purpose: Offers precise control for edits, making it suitable for larger areas.

- Function: Similar to the Spot Healing Brush, it samples surrounding pixels but grants the user more targeted selection capabilities.

3. **Clone Stamp Tool**
   - Purpose: Enables duplication of one image area and stamping it onto another, useful for removing objects or areas from an image.

4. **Patch Tool**
   - Purpose: Allows selection and replacement of a specific area with a similar part from elsewhere in the image, making it effective for addressing larger areas with complex textures.

5. **Content-Aware Move Tool**
   - Purpose: Empower users to relocate items in a picture while seamlessly filling the resulting void with content from the neighboring regions. This tool is adept at object removal and composition adjustments.

6. **Red Eye Tool**
   - Purpose: Speedily corrects red-eye issues in portraits by selecting the affected area and applying the necessary correction.

7. **Burn and Dodge Implements**
   - Purpose: These tools serve for selective brightening (Dodge) and darkening (Burn) of image areas, offering more nuanced control compared to global brightness and contrast adjustments.

8. **Smudge Tool**
   - Purpose: Blends colors and textures, imparting images with a softer, painterly appearance. It is also useful for skin retouching and smoothing.

9. Sharpen Tool
- Purpose: Enhances overall image sharpness and clarity by intensifying contrast along object edges, resulting in a sharper appearance.

10. Blur Tool
- Purpose: Softens or blurs an image, which can be valuable for achieving a shallow depth of field or addressing blemishes in portraits.

Painting Tools Group

The Painting Tools Group" includes a flexible selection of tools designed specifically for digital painting and sketching. With the assistance of these tools, users may easily create beautiful and realistic artwork. Let's examine the different instruments in this group and how they are used:

1. Brush Tool:
- **Purpose**: The brush tool is the cornerstone of digital painting, facilitating the application of strokes of color onto the canvas.

- **Function**: Users can customize the brush's size, opacity, and flow to achieve a variety of artistic effects.

2. **Pencil Tool**:
   - **Purpose**: The Pencil tool serves a function similar to the brush tool but creates crisp, hard-edged lines, making it ideal for precision and detailed drawings.

3. **Airbrush Tool**:
   - **Purpose**: The Airbrush Tool replicates the airbrushing technique, allowing users to spray color onto the canvas.
   - **Function**: Users can adjust parameters such as pressure, flow, and opacity to create smooth gradients and special effects.

4. **Eraser Tool**:
   - **Purpose**: The Eraser Tool enables users to selectively remove unwanted portions from their artwork or blend colors. In the most recent edition, users can choose from various eraser shapes for added control.

5. **Mixer Brush Tool**:
   - **Purpose**: This tool facilitates color blending on the canvas, mimicking traditional painting methods.
   - **Function**: Users can achieve a diverse range of blending effects by adjusting the tool's settings.

6. **Gradient Tool**:
   - **Purpose**: The Gradient Tool smoothly transitions between two or more colors and is frequently used for background creation, depth addition, and shading in illustrations.

7. **Pattern Stamp Tool**:
   - **Purpose**: This tool empowers users to paint with patterns rather than solid colors.

- **Function**: Users can select from a variety of built-in patterns or create their own to add unique textures to their artwork.
8. **Paint Bucket Tool**:
    - **Purpose**: The Paint Bucket Instrument expeditiously fills areas with solid colors or patterns, making it ideal for coloring large portions of an image.

Drawing Tools Group

The Drawing Tools Group comprises a versatile suite of digital art instruments that empower users to craft a diverse range of shapes, lines, and text elements within their designs. Artists, designers, and creators leverage these fundamental tools for producing captivating graphics, illustrations, and designs. The following details pertain to the individual tools that constitute the Drawing Tools Group:

1. **Pen Tool:**

    - **Function:** In Photoshop, the Pen Tool affords users the capability to meticulously craft curves and paths, delivering full control over the form and trajectory of their creations.
    - **Applications:** This tool finds extensive use in generating intricate designs, logos, and illustrations, enabling the creation of precisely tailored graphics.
2. **Shape Tools:**
    - **Function**: The Shape Tools provide users with the ability to generate fundamental geometric shapes such as rectangles, circles, polygons, and customized shapes within their compositions.

- **Utilization:** These tools offer an array of options for stroke, fill, and shape properties, enabling users to tailor these aspects and craft distinctive and visually striking designs.

3. **Line Tools:**
   - **Function:** The Line Tools facilitate the creation of both straight and curved lines, including dotted and dashed variations, to suit various design requirements.
   - **Utilization:** These tools prove invaluable in crafting technical illustrations, diagrams, and designs demanding precise and well-defined lines.

4. **Text Tool:**
   - **Function:** The Text Tool is dedicated to incorporating text elements into designs, granting users access to a wide spectrum of font options, font sizes, and text properties.
   - **Versatility**: It simplifies the creation of engaging, visually pleasing text-based designs by offering extensive flexibility in choosing and manipulating text attributes.

Selecting a tool accessible through the Toolbar

Choosing an instrument from the toolbar is a fundamental step in the image editing process. The toolbar serves as your gateway to a wide array of tools that facilitate image manipulation and enhancement. With each iteration of Photoshop, the toolbar undergoes enhancements to streamline the editing workflow and enhance user-friendliness.

The process of choosing an instrument from the toolbar begins with understanding the purpose of each tool. Hover your mouse cursor over an instrument from the toolbar, and a tooltip will appear, displaying the tool's name and a synopsis of its function. This feature is particularly beneficial for newcomers, as it provides clarity on the role of each tool and mitigates potential confusion.

After identifying the tool you wish to use, you can select it by selecting its corresponding icon within the toolbar. Alternatively, You can choose to employ keyboard shortcuts, which can significantly expedite your work, particularly for complex projects. The keyboard shortcuts are conveniently displayed beside All the tools within the toolbar, simplifying the process of memorization and utilization.

Adobe Photoshop 2024 offers several avenues for customizing the toolbar to align with your specific requirements. It is possible to reorganize the order of tool icons by simply clicking and dragging them, prioritizing easy access to frequently used tools. Right-clicking on the toolbar reveals a comprehensive list of all available tools within Photoshop. From this menu, you can add or remove tools by toggling the checkboxes beside their names.

An additional valuable feature of the toolbar is the double arrow situated near the base of the toolbar panel. Clicking this arrow unveils a set of hidden tools that may not fit within the visible toolbar space. This capability is particularly useful for streamlining the toolbar and keeping only the essential tools accessible.

In addition to tools for manipulating images and creation, the toolbar also incorporates options for canvas selection and navigation, including tools like the Hand tool and Zoom tool. These tools empower you to move, zoom in, or zoom out within your image, facilitating precise and efficient editing tasks.

Working with the Tool Properties

When working within Adobe Photoshop, the Tool Properties panel is essential for customizing and perfecting the tools you employ. This panel empowers you to adjust a plethora of settings and parameters for each tool, granting you enhanced command over your design projects and editing tasks.

To access the Tool Properties panel, navigate to "Windows" > "Tool Properties" in the menu bar, or you can swiftly summon it by pressing the "F4" key on your keyboard.

Once the panel is unveiled, it reveals a comprehensive list of all Photoshop's toolkits. Clicking on a specific tool activates its associated properties within the panel. While the properties available for adjustment may vary based on the selected tool, here are some common ones:

1. **Hardness and Size of Brush:** For painting and editing tools, you can finely tune the brush's size and hardness. Expanding the brush size covers a larger area while increasing hardness yields crisper edges.

2. **Opacity and Flow**: These settings regulate the tool's transparency and intensity. Lowering opacity or flow renders the tool more transparent and subtle while elevating these values makes it more solid and conspicuous.

3. **Blending Mode:** This setting dictates how the tool interacts with the existing colors on the canvas. A diverse array of blending modes, such as Normal, Multiply, Screen, and more, can be chosen to create distinct effects.

4. **Tool Presets**: Many tools within Photoshop come with predefined options, which can expedite your workflow by applying preset settings. You also have the liberty to save your own customized presets and access them within the panel.

5. **Specific Tool Options:** Certain tools boast unique properties put to their specific functions. For instance, using the Crop tool, you may manipulate the aspect ratio and resolution, while the Text tool enables adjustments like font selection, size, and character spacing. Beyond these core properties, the Tool Properties panel offers additional parameters for exploration, each contributing to diverse and dynamic effects. As you gain proficiency with Photoshop's toolbox, you'll uncover how these properties interplay with your designs and edits.

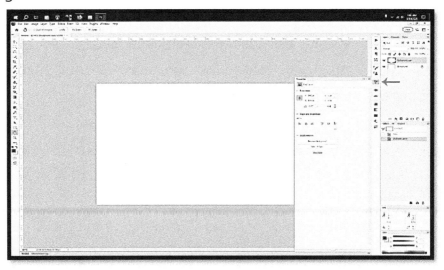

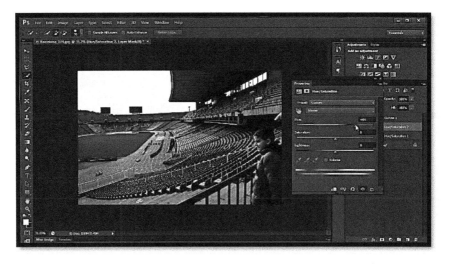

Understanding the Tool Properties within the Options Bar

One of the options is the Options Bar, which is a multifaceted tool that empowers you to explore various aspects of your work. It provides tool-specific options and properties that can significantly enhance your workflow and productivity. To fully grasp its functionality, let's explore the diverse elements within the Options Bar.

1. **Title Bar**: The Title Bar showcases the name of the currently open file in Photoshop. Clicking on it unveils a drop-down menu, offering options to create a new document, open existing files, or access recently opened files.

2. **Workspace Switcher**: The Workspace Switcher permits you to seamlessly transition between different workspaces, each tailored for specific tasks. Whether you're working on Essentials, Photography, Painting, or 3D projects, you can effortlessly switch to an optimized set of tools and panels.

3. **Tools Presets**: Tools Presets come in handy for saving and loading specific tool settings. If you have preferred tool configurations that you frequently use, this feature enables you to maintain consistency and efficiency.

4. **History and Snapshot Panel**: The History Panel maintains a record of your actions, enabling you to undo or redo specific changes. Snapshots allow you to save various versions of your work, facilitating experimentation and side-by-side comparisons.

5. **Tool Options**: Tool Options present a range of properties related to the currently selected tool. You can fine-tune attributes like brush size, blending, opacity, and many options, customizing them to meet your exact needs.

6. **Alignment and Distribution Options**: When you have multiple layers selected, the Alignment and Distribution Options come into play. They empower you to Arrange and disperse the layers. Based on different criteria, including space and object edges.

7. **Show Options**: Show Options introduce additional features specific to particular tools. For instance, when making use of the Crop tool, these options enable you to specify the crop's aspect ratio or toggle the visibility of the crop shield.

8. **Document Options**: Document Options are dedicated to the current document and encompass elements like color mode, resolution, and canvas dimensions. These settings prove invaluable when preparing an image for print or web usage.

9. **Workspace Options**: Workspace Options grant you the flexibility to customize the appearance and layout of your workspace. Furthermore, you can save and load custom workspaces, tailoring your environment to suit diverse tasks or projects.

Using the Status Bar

The Status Bar is situated at the bottom of the program window and serves as a valuable source of information about your current project and available tools. It plays an important role in aiding your navigation and ensuring the smooth execution of your tasks. To maximize your use of the Status Bar, consider the following tips:

1. **Review Document Details:** The Status Bar provides essential insights into your active document, including details like file format, color mode, and dimensions. You can also monitor and adjust the current zoom level by clicking the percentage value and inputting a new value.

2. **Utilize the Zoom Slider:** You can seamlessly zoom in and out of your document using the slider on the right side of the Status Bar. A simple leftward or rightward drag of the slider enables you to zoom out or in, respectively.

3. **Monitor Cursor Coordinates**: The Status Bar displays the precise cursor coordinates relative to your document. This feature proves particularly beneficial when working on projects that require exacting precision in designs and measurements.

4. **Access Hidden Tools:** The Status Bar conceals some valuable tools that may not be immediately visible in the standard Photoshop interface. To access them, simply right-click on the Status Bar and select the desired tool, such as the Ruler or Eyedropper.

5. **Customize Status Bar Content:** You can customize the content displayed within the Status Bar to your specific needs. By right-clicking on the Status Bar and choosing "Customize Status Bar," you can access a menu where you can choose the things you wish to have visible.

6. **Leverage the Progress Bar:** When applying filters or other effects to your image, the Status Bar may feature a progress bar. This bar offers real-time updates on the effect's progress, including an estimate of the remaining time for completion.

7. **Access Quick Help:** The Status Bar conveniently incorporates a search bar that enables you to pose questions or seek assistance regarding Photoshop. This feature promptly retrieves helpful articles and resources from Adobe's knowledge base.

Getting used to Photoshop panels

1. **Explore the Panels:** Begin your journey with Photoshop panels by taking some time to explore them. Familiarize yourself with

the purpose and functions of each panel. Understanding the role of each panel will significantly enhance your ability to efficiently use Photoshop.

2. **Customize Your Workspace**: Photoshop provides the flexibility to customize your workspace by adjusting panel positions and sizes to match your preferences. Rearrange the panels to create a workspace that aligns with your workflow by dragging and clicking them to your desired location.

3. **Use Shortcuts**: To expedite your workflow, learn keyboard shortcuts for frequently used panels. For instance, you can open the Brushes panel with "F5" or the Layers panel with "F6." A list of shortcuts is located in the Photoshop menu under Edit > Keyboard Shortcuts.

4. **Learn the Essentials:** Some panels are indispensable for most Photoshop tasks, including Layers, Color, and Tools panels. If you're new to Photoshop, dedicate time to getting acquainted with these fundamental panels.

5. **Use Panels in Groups**: Organize your workspace effectively by grouping multiple panels. To create a panel group, simply click and drag one panel to the tab of another panel, then let go of the mouse. This creates a collapsible or expandable group for convenient access.

6. **Save Custom Workspaces**: If you possess a specific panel arrangement that suits your needs, save it as a custom workspace. This feature allows you to switch between different workspaces according to your current task. To save a custom workspace, navigate to Open > Workspace > Create New Workspace.

7. **Use the Tab Key:** The Tab key is a handy tool to toggle the visibility of all panels, enabling you to focus solely on your

artwork without distractions. You can also utilize the Shift + Tab shortcut to show or hide only the toolbar and side panels.

8. **Utilize Panel Menus**: Most panels offer a small menu icon in the top right corner, granting access to supplementary options and features. This is valuable for customizing the panel or uncovering hidden functionalities.

9. **Experiment with Different Views:** Customize your panel views to accommodate your tastes. You can collapse a panel to display only its name or icons or expand it to reveal its full content. Additionally, you can switch between different presets using the "Essentials" drop-down menu located in the top-right corner of the panels.

10. **Practice and Learn**: Becoming proficient with Photoshop panels requires time and practice. The more you engage with Photoshop, the more at ease you will become with the panels. Dedicate time to experiment and discover new features, continuously improving your skills and workflow.

Expanding, Resizing, and Collapsing Panels

Expanding, resizing, and collapsing panels play a role in the organization and customization of your workspace. These functions empower you to put the size and arrangement of various panels to align according to your tastes and requirements.

When you expand a panel, you effectively enlarge it, revealing a more comprehensive array of options and controls nested within. You can achieve this expansion by either clicking on the arrow icon situated at the top-right corner of the panel or by executing a double-click on the panel's tab. This feature comes in rather handy when you need additional space to access the full spectrum of tools and settings contained within a specific panel.

Resizing a panel, nevertheless, in contrast, involves the adjustment of its width or height to accommodate your screen or to better suit the amount of content it holds. To resize a panel, you can simply click and drag its edges to your desired dimensions. Alternatively, you can right-click on the panel tab and choose the "Resize Panel" option to input precise measurements. This level of flexibility allows you to tailor your workspace to prioritize the panels most integral to your workflow.

Collapsing a panel refers to the process of minimizing it into its tab form or concealing it entirely from view. This feature comes in rather handy when you seek to reclaim screen space or when a particular panel is temporarily unnecessary. Collapsing a panel can be accomplished with the arrow icon at the panel's top-right corner, double-clicking the tab, or right-clicking the panel tab and selecting "Collapse Panel Group" to minimize a cluster of panels.

In addition to these actions, you can rearrange panels by clicking and dragging their tabs to different positions within your workspace. This function enables you to group panels that are related or place frequently used panels within easy reach.

Furthermore, you can establish multiple custom workspaces by leveraging the expand, resize, and collapse panel functions to suit your individual needs. This empowers you to optimize your workflow by granting quick access to the panels and tools you rely on most frequently, ultimately enhancing your efficiency and productivity.

Making it right with Undo and Redo Commands

In the realm of creative software the Undo and Redo commands stand as indispensable tools that offer the means to swiftly rectify or revert alterations made in your creative process, affording you the chance to "set things right" within your workflow. The Undo command serves as a direct route to countermanding your most recent action. This can be accomplished by navigating to Edit > Undo or utilizing the keyboard shortcuts "Ctrl+Z" on Windows or "Command+Z" on Mac. This command is versatile, permitting multiple sequential uses to reverse multiple steps in your editing journey.

Conversely, the Redo command, which is accessible through Edit > Redo or via the keyboard shortcuts "Ctrl+Shift+Z" on Windows and "Command+Shift+Z" on Mac, enables you to revisit previously undone actions. This functionality proves valuable when you inadvertently undo a modification or experience a change of heart regarding a prior action.

Nonetheless, it is essential to know the limitations of these commands. For instance, when you apply the Undo command after making several consecutive changes, it reverts you to the preceding step, discarding all alterations made beyond that point. Consequently, if you wish to modify something done a few steps back, you must redo all the intervening actions.

To extract the utmost utility from the instructions for Undo and Redo in Adobe Photoshop 2024, strategic integration within your workflow is paramount. This strategy encompasses regular saving of your work to create multiple checkpoints for potential reversions. Furthermore, Photoshop's History panel offers a comprehensive record of all steps taken in your editing process, simplifying navigation to a specific point when required.

Erasing editing steps with the History Box

The History Panel serves as an important tool for overseeing and reversing editing actions. It empowers users to effortlessly navigate the sequence of modifications applied to an image and rectify any undesired alterations.

Use these procedures to remove particular editing activity as shown in the History Panel:

1. **Open the Panel of History:** To access the History Panel, navigate to Window > History.

2. **Select the editing actions for removal**: Within the History Panel, click on the action you wish to remove. To select multiple actions, hold down the CTRL/CMD key while clicking on your chosen steps.

3. **Eliminate or modify the selected actions**: Right-click on the selected editing actions and select the desired option. As an example, you can opt for "Delete" to completely remove the actions, or "Clear to this point" to retain only the selected actions while discarding those that follow.

4. **Confirm the changes:** A pop-up window will prompt you to confirm the changes. Click "Yes" to proceed.

5. **Removal of the selected editing actions:** The deleted actions will no longer be visible Within the Historical Panel, and the image will revert to its state before the execution of those actions.

It is important to bear in mind that once you eliminate editing actions from the History Panel, they cannot be recovered. It is advisable to duplicate the picture before implementing any changes in case you need to revert to a prior version.

Managing the History Box

Effectively managing the history functionality empowers you to monitor your project's evolution and facilitates the option to return to previous project versions. Here are some valuable tips for optimizing your usage of the history feature:

1. **Activate the History Panel:** Open the Panel of History by navigating to View > Historical. This will unveil a panel at the right corner of your workspace, presenting a chronological record of your project's history.

2. **Set the Number of States**: By default, Photoshop grants you up to 50 history states, allowing you to retrace 50 steps from your current project state. You can customize this count by visiting Preferences > Performance and adjusting the History States setting. Be mindful that a higher number of states will consume more memory.

3. **Employ Snapshots:** The snapshot feature enables you to preserve specific project milestones within your history. This proves beneficial for comparing different versions or creating multiple project variations.

4. **Assign Descriptive Names to History States:** Enhance clarity by renaming your history states. A simple double-click on a state within the history panel allows you to provide labels that elucidate the changes made at each state.

5. **Leverage the History Brush:** Using the History Brush affords the capability to revisit a specific project state and selectively apply it to a particular area. This is invaluable when you wish to make adjustments to a specific segment of your project without impacting the entirety.

6. **Revert to a Prior State**: To return to an earlier project state, Choose the preferred state within the history panel suffices. This action resets your project to the chosen state.
7. **Clear Your History:** If you aim to reduce your project's file size or initiate a fresh start without a cluttered history, proceed to Modify > Eliminate > History. This action will clear all states and images of history, providing a clean slate for your creative work.

Setting Photoshop Preferences

Photoshop preferences serve as Configurable settings that allow users to personalize the software's look and feel to suit their preferences and requirements. To access these preferences, navigate to "select the "Edit" option, and select "Preferences" or utilize the keyboard shortcut "Cmd/Ctrl + K." Preferences encompass diverse categories, including general, interface, file handling, performance, and more. Within each category, users have the flexibility to fine-tune aspects such as the unit of measurement, color configurations, grid, and guide settings, and default file-saving preferences. Furthermore, these preferences can be saved and imported into other Photoshop installations, streamlining the process of maintaining preferred settings across multiple devices.

Working with Cloud Documents

Photoshop provides users with the capability to work seamlessly with cloud documents, simplifying the process of file management and access. Here's a summary of how to navigate cloud documents:

1. **Setting Up Cloud Storage:** To initiate your interaction with cloud documents. You'll need a Creative Cloud account. If you don't have one, it's easy to sign up for a free account. Once you have your

Creative Cloud account, activate your cloud storage by navigating to Edit > Preferences > General. Check the boxes for "Sync Settings" and "Enable Auto Save to Creative Cloud."

2. **Uploading and Saving Files to Cloud**: To upload and save your files to cloud storage, select the "Cloud documents" option from the Home screen, or choose File > Save as > Cloud documents. This enables direct saving to the cloud, granting access to your files from any device linked to your Creative Cloud account.

3. **Syncing Files**: Whenever you alter your cloud documents, Photoshop automatically saves and syncs those modifications to the cloud. If you are engaged in a file that someone else has accessed, Photoshop will notify you and offer the option to synchronize the changes or open it in read-only mode.

4. **Collaborating on Cloud Documents:** Photoshop facilitates collaborative efforts on cloud documents, streamlining teamwork on a single file. You can invite other Creative Cloud users to collaborate on your cloud documents by choosing the "Collaborate" option via the Home screen or by clicking the "Invite collaborators" button within the file's properties.

5. **Accessing Cloud Documents on Mobile:** One of the notable advantages of cloud documents is the capacity to access and edit your files while on the move, courtesy of the Photoshop mobile app. Simply log in with your account on Creative Cloud on the mobile app, and you will gain access to all your cloud documents.

6. **Organizing Your Cloud Documents:** Photoshop dedicates a tab to "Cloud documents" on the Home screen, simplifying the organization and management of your cloud files. You can conveniently sort your documents by name, date modified, or size.

Additionally, the option to create folders enhances your file organization capabilities.

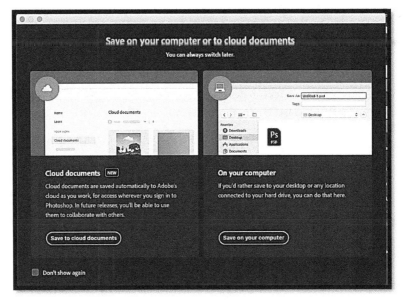

CHAPTER THREE

FEATURES OF ADOBE PHOTOSHOP 2024

The Future of Photoshop: Generative AI

For over three decades, Adobe Photoshop has maintained its position as a pioneering tool in digital image editing, continually evolving to meet the ever-changing demands of the creative industry. As technology continues to advance, shaping the future of design, the question arises: What will Adobe Photoshop look like in 2024?

Generative AI, also known as artificial intelligence, is an evolving technology with the capacity to completely transform the creative process in various ways. It leverages algorithms and machine learning to generate new content and automate tasks traditionally undertaken by humans.

One of the areas where generative AI will wield a profound impact is in automating tedious and time-consuming tasks. Instead of manually erasing an unwanted object from an image, generative AI will possess the capability to automatically detect and replace it with nearby pixels of a similar nature. This revolutionary capability will save designers countless hours, enabling them to channel their efforts into more creativity-driven tasks.

Generative Fill is a revolutionary and enchanting feature within Adobe Photoshop, driven by the innovative collection of generative AI driven by Firefly. Capabilities. It taps into your inherent creativity, allowing you to non-destructively enlarge, reduce, or add content to your photos by using straightforward text prompts, available in more than a hundred languages.

This remarkable tool seamlessly aligns with your image's viewpoint, illumination, and fashion, transforming previously laborious tasks into enjoyable endeavors. It delivers realistic outcomes that will astonish, amaze, and delight you within moments.

The newly generated content is placed within a dedicated Generative layer, providing a vast playground of creative possibilities. It enables you to effortlessly revert to the original state without affecting your initial image. This empowers you to harness the strength and accuracy of Photoshop to elevate your image to levels that exceed even your anticipations.

Photoshop's Generic Fill feature draws its power from Adobe Firefly, now accessible for business usage. This assurance underscores your creative process, as Firefly is a family of generative AI models deliberately crafted to meet commercial standards, ensuring that you can explore the outer limits of your creativity with confidence. Firefly's training is enriched by Adobe Stock's vast collection of hundreds of millions of high-resolution, licensed, professional-caliber photos, renowned for their exceptional superiority in the marketplace.

Generative Fill empowers you to:

1. **Generate objects**: Choose a region within your image, and with a textual prompt, craft or substitute objects seamlessly.
2. **Generate backgrounds**: Select the backdrop behind your subject and utilize a text prompt to generate an entirely new scene.
3. **Expand images**: Enlarge your image's canvas, and by selecting the vacant area, create a seamless expansion. Utilizing no prompt yields a harmonious extension, while employing a prompt adds content while expanding the scene.
4. **Remove objects**: Effortlessly remove selected objects by producing without request and witness them vanish seamlessly.

Generate an Object

1. **Choosing a Region**: To start, you select a specific area within an existing image. This region can be as small as a single element in the image or cover a larger portion, depending on your creative intent.

2. **Textual Prompt**: Once the region is chosen, you provide a textual prompt. This is where you describe what you wish to change or add inside the designated space. The prompt acts as an instruction to the generative algorithm, guiding it on what kind of object you wish to create or modify.

3. **Seamless Craft or Replacement:** The magic happens as the algorithm interprets your prompt and generates the desired object seamlessly within the chosen region. This object can be entirely new, matching your description, or it might be a replacement for an existing element in the image. The goal is to make the addition

or replacement appear as if it were part of the original composition, maintaining visual cohesion and harmony.

Generate Back Ground

Choose the background that goes behind the subject or the portion of your picture where you wish to insert a new scene first. This is the canvas where you will create a new backdrop image.

Wait for the Contextual Task Bar to appear to utilize the Generative Fill feature. Usually, when you work with a picture in Photoshop, this occurs.

From the Contextual Task Bar, choose "Generative Fill". You will be prompted to select this choice by an on-screen notice If you've never done this before utilizing the feature.

Expand Images

- **Canvas Enlargement**: With the assistance of this tool, you can essentially extend the borders of your image by making the canvas larger. This expansion may occur in both height and width. You'll have more room to collaborate with or to smoothly incorporate new stuff into the picture if you do this.

- **Choose the Unoccupied Area**: Once the canvas has been expanded, you can choose the newly formed unoccupied area. The location of the expansion will be decided by this choice. It's similar to directing the growth of the image.

- **Using No Prompt for Harmonic Extension:** Generative Fill will attempt to produce a harmonic extension of your current scene into the designated space if you decide to enlarge your image without utilizing a textual prompt. The chosen space will be harmoniously expanded using Generative Fill to build your current scene. The purpose of this extension is to make the image look as though it was taken with those extended parts originally, by blending in perfectly with the surrounding information.

- **Using a cue for Content Addition:** In contrast, Generative Fill will enlarge the image and add certain content to the expanded area if you decide to provide a textual cue. The generative algorithm will follow your text prompt to produce information that is relevant to your description. These could be scenes, items, or aspects that fit in naturally with the picture. For instance, if you own any picture of a cityscape and you want to enlarge it using a prompt like "Extend the skyline with additional skyscrapers," Generative Fill will create new skyscrapers that mix in perfectly with the existing cityscape in addition to enlarging the skyline.

- **Seamless Integration**: The way the extended content and the original image are seamlessly integrated is essential to this function. The goal is for the output to seem as though it was a part of the original composition, regardless of whether you decide to add content with a prompt or to expand harmoniously without one. This guarantees the preservation of the image's artistic coherence and integrity.

Remove Objects

1. **Object Selection**: To initiate the object removal process, begin by choosing the specific object or element within your image that you wish to eliminate. This can be any unwanted element, such as a

person, a background element, or an object that you desire to erase from the scene.

2. **Generating Without a Prompt**: Unlike the previous sections that involved adding or expanding content, object removal in Generative Fill can be done seamlessly without requiring a textual prompt. This means that you're not required to provide any specific instructions on what should replace the removed object.

3. **Seamless Object Removal**: Once you initiate the generation process without a prompt, the Generative Fill algorithm works to remove the selected object from your image. This removal is designed to seamlessly blend the surrounding pixels, creating an image that appears as if the object was never there. The result is a visually coherent and aesthetically pleasing composition.

Removing objects using Generative Fill offers a hassle-free method to clean up images and enhance their visual appeal. Whether you're removing distractions from a photograph or editing out unwanted elements, this feature simplifies the process and ensures that the final image maintains its integrity and quality. It's a valuable tool for both professional image editors and casual users looking to improve their pictures.

Using Photoshop to Generate Credits

Generative credits are a valuable currency that can be utilized across a range of generative AI features with Adobe Firefly as its power source within the applications you're entitled to use. It's crucial to remember that these generative credits reset every month, ensuring ongoing access to creative capabilities. If you have multiple subscriptions, your total generative credits available will be the sum of what's included in each plan.

The subscription has been enhanced to provide the following methods of accessing generative AI creations:

- **Subscription fees for Creative Cloud and Adobe Stock**: These packages include a certain quantity of generative AI products each month, like vector drawings or standard-resolution photos generated by Adobe Firefly. You can use generative AI activities after you've used up all of your monthly allotment of generative credits, but generative AI features might not function as well.

- **Paid Plans for Adobe Express and Adobe Firefly:** A certain number of monthly generative AI creations using vector graphics or standard-resolution photos driven by Adobe Firefly are also included in these programs. You may still produce vector drawings or standard-resolution photos using two generative AI actions each day after you've used all your monthly allotment of generative credits until your credits reset the next month.

- **The free plans for Adobe Creative Cloud, Adobe Firefly, and Adobe Express:** A certain quantity of generative AI works, including vector graphics or standard-resolution photos driven by Adobe Firefly, are provided to users on these free plans each month. You can continue creating assets with Firefly-powered features by upgrading to a premium plan once you've reached the plan-specific generative credit limit. As an alternative, you can put off starting your creative projects until the next month when your generating credits refresh.

When do generative credits renew?

In the case of paying subscribers, generating credits are renewed on the first of each month following the plan's billing schedule. Your generating credits will reset on the 15th of each consecutive month, for instance, if your plan started on the 15th of that month. Generative credits are awarded to free users without a paid subscription following their first usage of a Firefly-powered service. For example, a free user will be awarded 25 generative credits upon initially logging onto the Firefly website and using a tool such as Text to Image. These credits have a one-month expiration period from the date of allocation. The credits will run out on the fifteenth of the following month if the first usage takes place on that day. New generating credits are allocated in the following months upon the first usage of a Firefly-powered function. These credits have a one-month expiration date once they are allocated. The credits will expire on the 19th of the following month if the first usage in the second month occurs on that date. Regardless of when they initially access them, our method guarantees that customers have a full month for their allotment of generating credits.

How do you use generating credits?

The utilization of productive credits is contingent on two factors: the computational complexity of the generated output and the specific generative AI feature employed.

Here are instances where generative credits are deducted:

- Initiating the "Generate" action within Text Effects.

- Selecting " "Refresh" or "Load more" is available in Text to Image.

For Adobe Illustrator, generative credits are consumed when you:

- Utilize Using Adobe Illustrator, select "Generative Recolor."

For Adobe Express, generative credits are consumed when you:

- Employ In Adobe Express, select "Text Effects.

In Adobe Photoshop, generative credits are utilized when you:

- Make use of Adobe Photoshop, and select "Generative Fill."

However, generative credits are not deducted in the following cases:

- When utilizing generative AI features categorized as "0" in the rate table.
- When selecting "View samples" in the Firefly gallery, viewing the existing artwork doesn't trigger a new generation. Generative credits are only debited when opting for "Refresh," which necessitates generating new content.

This credit system ensures that Amounts of generating credits are assigned based on the complexity of the task and the feature used, enabling users to effectively manage their credit consumption.

Tools, Options, and Contextual Taskbar

Select a tool

The panel for Tools is located on the left side of the Photoshop application screen.

Within this panel, each tool offers additional options that are displayed in the context-sensitive options bar. To access these supplementary features, simply click on the small triangle located at the lower right of the tool icon.

For further information about each tool, including their names and other details, hover your pointer over them. This action will provide you with valuable insights into the tools at your disposal.

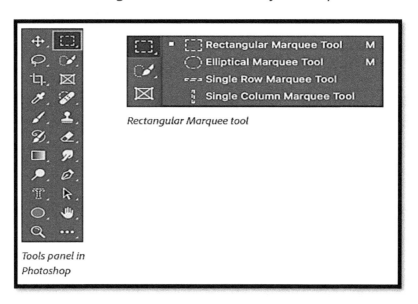

Rectangular Marquee tool

Tools panel in
Photoshop

To select a tool

1. Pick a Tool

2. Take any of the subsequent actions:

a. Opt for a tool from the Tools panel. If a small triangle appears at the lower right corner of the tool, keep the mouse button pressed. To reveal additional button tools, and then select the specific tool you wish to use.

b. Alternatively,

Employ the tool's designated keyboard shortcut. The keyboard shortcut is conveniently displayed in the tool's tooltip. For instance, you can choose the Move tool by simply pressing 'V.'

NB: To quickly switch to a different tool, press and hold a keyboard shortcut key. Photoshop automatically switches back to the tool you were using before the brief changeover as soon as you press the shortcut key.

Cycle through hidden tools

Let's go into more detail on how to alter this behavior in Photoshop and how to cycle between the tools:

By holding down Shift and repeatedly clicking a tool shortcut key, you may cycle between a set of hidden tools by default.

1. **Default Behavior**: When using Photoshop, you can quickly switch between a set of related tools by holding down the keyboard's Shift key and then repeatedly pressing the shortcut key associated with the desired tool. For example, when working with brush-related tools, pressing the B key will choose the Brush tool. However, if you continue to press B while holding down Shift, you'll cycle through related tools like The Pen Tool the Color Replacement Tool, and more.

2. **Efficient Tool Selection**: This default behavior is designed to streamline your workflow. It enables you to access and switch between tools that share a similar category or function, simplifying it to find the specific tool you need without returning to the Tools panel.

You may disable this choice if you'd rather cycle between the tools without having to hold down Shift:

1. **Customizing the Behavior**: Photoshop provides users with the flexibility to tailor the tool-switching behavior to their preferences.

2. **Access Preferences**: To change this setting, navigate to the "Preferences" menu. On Windows, you'll find it under "Edit > Preferences > General," while on macOS, it's located under "Photoshop > Preferences > General."

3. **Disable Shift Key Requirement**: Within the Preferences menu, look for an option labeled "Use Shift Key for Tool Switch." This option, when checked, enforces the default behavior of requiring the Shift key to cycle through related tools.

4. **Select the Option**: "Use Shift Key for Tool Switch" may be unchecked or deselected to cycle among tools without holding down Shift.

5. **Save Your Preferences**: After making this change, ensure you save your preferences. Your selected tool-switching behavior will now be in effect.

Change Tool Pointers

Every default pointer in Photoshop has a unique hotspot, which is the specific point where a result or activity begins in the image. For many tools, you can choose to change to the exact pointers, which manifest as crosshairs in the vicinity of the hotspot.

Here's how you can customize your tool pointers:

1. **Select Pointer Preferences**: By default, the tool's pointing device is often identical to the tool's icon, which you observe after choosing the tool. For instance, the marquee tools default to the crosshair pointer, the text tool to the I-beam, and the painting tools to the symbol for brush size.

2. **Access Preferences**: To adjust these settings, go to the "Preferences" menu. On Windows, it can be found under "Edit >

Preferences > Cursors," and on macOS, it's located under "Photoshop > Preferences > Cursors."

3. **Choose Pointer Settings**: Within the Cursors section, you can select the settings that suit your preferences beneath "Painting Cursors" and "Other Cursors." After making your choices, click "OK."

- **Standard**: This setting shows arrows as tool icons, matching the default appearance.
- **Precise**: Opting for this setting displays pointers as crosshairs, providing precise control by showing the exact center point of your tool's effect.
- **Normal Brush Tip**: With this option, the tool's affected area is approximately half the size of the pointer outline. It draws attention to the pixels that would be most noticeable. Impacted by the tool.
- **Full-Size Brush Tip**: This setting makes the pointer outline match almost all of the regions that the gadget will impact. It essentially encompasses every pixel that would influenced by the tool.
- **Display Crosshair on Brush Point**: Selecting this option displays crosshairs in the brush shape's middle, offering enhanced guidance.
- **When painting, only display the crosshair**: If you're working with large brushes, this option can improve performance by showing only the crosshair during painting.

The choices for Painting Cursors govern the appearance of guidelines for the following instruments:

- Eraser

- Pencil

- Paintbrush

- Healing Brush

- Clone Stamp

- Pattern Stamp

- Quick Selection

- Smudge

- Blur

- Sharpen

- Dodge

- Burn

- Sponge

The Other Cursors settings control the arrows for the subsequent instruments:

- Marquee

- Lasso

- Polygonal Lasso

- Magic Wand

- Crop

- Slice

- Patch

- Eyedropper

- Pen

- Gradient

- Line

- Paint Bucket

- Magnetic Lasso

- Magnetic Pen

- Freeform Pen

- Measure

- Color Sampler

Resize or alter the painting cursor's hardness visually.

To visually adjust the size or sturdiness of cursor painting, take these actions:

1. Resize the Cursor: To change the size of the cursor, press Alt and right-click (Windows) or Control and Option (macOS), then drag it left or right.

2. Modify Hardness: To alter the hardness of the cursor, simply drag it up or down.

As you make these adjustments, the painting cursor will dynamically reflect your changes, providing a real-time preview of the cursor's size and hardness. Please note that these previews require OpenGL. This feature allows for more precise control when working with various painting tools in Photoshop.

Tool options bar

The Tool Options Bar is located just beneath the workspace's menu bar. Is a dynamic element in Photoshop, It adjusts based on the active tool selection, offering context-specific settings. While some settings like opacity and painting modes are shared across multiple tools, others are unique to specific tools.

You can easily reposition the Toolbar Options within the workspace using the grip bar, and you have the flexibility to dock it either at the top or bottom of the display. Toolmarks conveniently appear when you hover your arrow over an instrument. To make the Tool Options Bar visible or invisible, open the "Window" menu and select "Options." For any tool, you can swiftly restore its default settings. Simply right-click (on Windows) or control-click (on macOS) Select "Reset Tool" or "Reset All Tools" from the context menu by clicking on the tool icon in the Tool Options Bar.

This versatile element in Photoshop, The Tool Options Bar guarantees that you can easily to the relevant settings for your selected tools and the ability to restore default configurations with ease.

Contextual Taskbar

The Task Bar in Context is a dynamic and persistent menu designed to streamline your workflow by offering the most pertinent next steps based on your current actions. For instance, when you've selected an object, the Contextual Task Bar will emerge directly on the canvas, providing a curated set of options for your potential next actions. These may include actions such as Create Adjustment Layer, Fill Selection, Feather, Invert, and Select and Mask, put to enhance your workflow.

To disable this feature, which is activated by default, you can go to "Window > Contextual Task Bar."

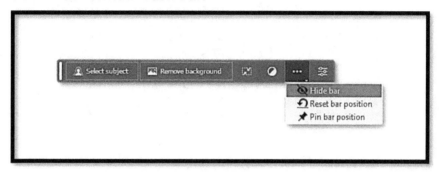

New Document workflow

When you initiate the creation of a new document in Photoshop, you'll encounter the Contextual Task Bar, designed especially to help you navigate the procedure. When you launch a new, blank document from the Photoshop home screen, this taskbar appears. Or by navigating to "File > New."

The "New Document Workflow" bar is an intuitive and dynamic feature that assists you in configuring your new document. It provides a set of context-sensitive options, simplifying it to define the essential parameters of your project. These options may include specifying dimensions, resolution, color mode, background content, and much more.

In essence, the "New Document Workflow" bar serves as your helpful companion when starting a new project in Photoshop. It ensures that you have access to the most relevant options for your document creation process, thus simplifying your initial setup and enhancing your overall efficiency.

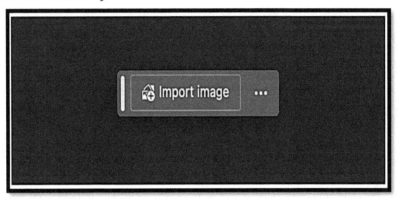

Open Image/File workflow

The "Open Image/File Workflow" is a user-friendly feature in Photoshop that comes into play when you're accessing and working with existing image files. This taskbar is specifically designed to assist you in streamlining the process of opening image files, ensuring you have access to essential tools and options as you work with your files. It becomes visible in the following scenarios:

1. **Accessing from the Home Screen**: When you open an existing image or file from the Photoshop home screen, you'll notice the "Open Image/File Workflow" bar. This is particularly useful when you're returning to a project you've been working on or when you want to continue editing an image that you've previously saved.
2. **File > Open**: You can also access this taskbar when you use the "File > Open" option to open image files. Whether you're opening

local files from your computer or accessing files from a cloud-based storage service, this workflow ensures that you have a set of context-sensitive options at your disposal.

The "Open Image/File Workflow" is context-aware, meaning it adapts to your specific needs depending on the file you're opening. It provides you with quick access to features like image adjustments, layer management, and transformation tools, all of which are particularly relevant when working with pre-existing images or files.

Type tool workflow

The "Type Tool Workflow" is a context-sensitive feature in Photoshop that is activated when you choose to use the toolbar's Type tool and proceed to create a text box on the canvas. This workflow is specifically designed to assist you in the process of adding and formatting text within your Photoshop projects.

Here's a detailed breakdown of how this workflow operates:

1. **Selecting the Type Tool:** When you opt for the Type tool from the toolbar, you are indicating your intention to add text to your project. This is a pivotal step as it initiates the Type Tool Workflow.

2. **Drawing a Text Box**: After selecting the Type tool, you can create a text box by simply dragging and clicking on the canvas to define the area where your text will be placed. This text box provides a designated space for your text content.

3. **Activation of the Workflow Bar**: Once you've drawn the text box, the "Type Tool Workflow" bar automatically appears on the screen. This taskbar is context-aware, meaning it offers a range of options and settings that are directly relevant to the functioning procedure with text.

The "Type Tool Workflow" bar offers various functions and settings, including options for font selection, text size, alignment, character and paragraph formatting, and more. It simplifies the task of adding and customizing text within your project by providing quick and intuitive access to the necessary tools and settings.

Selection's workflow

Let's go over the details of this bar's appearance and operation, which includes the ability to adjust a selection, make a mask, and apply the Generative Fill function:

Appearance and Context: The bar in question appears under specific circumstances in Photoshop. It becomes active after you have made a selection within your image or document. This selection can involve choosing a region of the image, isolating an object, or defining a particular area of interest. Once your selection is in place, the bar appears, offering you a set of useful options to further enhance your selected area.

Refining Selection: One of the primary functions of this bar is to provide tools and settings that enable you to improve the quality of your choice. This can be especially valuable when working with complex or intricate selections. You can fine-tune and adjust the edges of your selection to ensure that it precisely encompasses the area you intend to work on.

Creating Masks: In addition to selection refinement, the bar allows you to create masks. Masks are essential for non-destructive editing in Photoshop. By using the options in this bar, you can convert your selection into a mask. Masks allow you to control the visibility and impact of various elements within your image or project, making it easier to apply edits or effects selectively.

Generative Fill Feature: Furthermore, this bar provides access to the Generative Fill feature. Once your selection is made, you have the option to employ to add material to the chosen region, using Generative Fill. This powerful feature uses AI to generate and fill in content based on your selection or prompts, offering creative possibilities for image enhancement and manipulation.

Menu with more options

To view more Photoshop taskbar options, take the following actions:

1. **Click the Three-Dot Icon:** Locate and Click the three-dot symbol. On the taskbar. This action will open an additional options menu, providing you with several choices for managing the taskbars.

2. **Hide the Bar:** Should you wish your screens contextual task bars should all be removed. Choose the "Hide bar" option from the menu. This action will conceal all active task bars. You can later select "Window > Contextual Task Bar" to reopen them.

3. **Reset Bar Position:** Designed to accompany you while you work on your canvas, the Contextual Task Bar puts pertinent tools at your fingertips. Use the "Reset bar position" option found in the "more options menu" to move the bar back to its original location allows you to readjust the task bar's placement to suit your workflow.

4. **Pin Bar Position:** The "Pin bar position" option enables you to fix the taskbar in its current location, ensuring it remains in place as you work. This not only applies to the current bar but also to all subsequent bars in the way you work. Unpin a bar by simply deselecting the "Pin bar position" option from the "More options menu.

Masking workflow

The "Masking Workflow" is a crucial aspect of image editing and manipulation in Photoshop. It comes into play when you're working with masks, be it in the Workspace for Select and Mask when you're creating a mask chosen from the array, or selecting the thumbnail of a layer mask. Here's a detailed overview of this workflow:

Context and Appearance: The "Masking Workflow" becomes active when you enter the Select and Mask workspace, indicating that you are about to fine-tune a mask for a specific element within your image. It also triggers when you make a mask with a variety, allowing you to isolate and manipulate portions of your image, or when you select a layer mask thumbnail for an existing mask within your layers.

Refining Masks: The primary purpose of this workflow is to provide you with a variety of instruments and options to refine your masks. You can utilize the tools to add or subtract areas from your masked region, allowing for precise control over which parts of the image are visible or hidden. This is essential for achieving complex and intricate masking effects in your projects.

View Mode Options: The "Masking Workflow" offers various view mode options. These options enable you to visualize and assess the mask's impact on your image in real-time. You can toggle between different view modes to see how your mask interacts with the underlying content, making it easier to achieve the desired result.

Modifying Mask Properties: You also can modify mask properties such as density and feather. Adjusting the density controls the opacity of the masked area while feathering enables the creation of seamless transitions between the masked and unmasked regions. These properties play a critical role in achieving seamless and natural-looking mask effects.

Generative Expand workflow

This specific bar becomes active whenever you select and utilize the Crop tool. It is a context-sensitive element that emerges to facilitate your cropping process. Whether you're resizing or adjusting the composition of your image, this bar offers options tailored to the Crop tool's functions.

The primary functions of this bar include options to straighten your image and adjust the aspect ratio. Straightening is especially beneficial for aligning horizons or correcting skewed perspectives in your photos. Adjusting the aspect ratio allows you to define specific proportions for your cropped area, ensuring it conforms to your intended dimensions.

In addition to cropping, the bar provides an option to utilize the functionality called Generative Expand. This feature is especially valuable when you choose to expand the canvas rather than cropping it. It enables you to seamlessly extend your image, and you can apply the Generative Fill feature to generate content for the newly added areas, harmoniously blending them with the existing composition.

Tool Presets

Tool presets are a convenient feature in Photoshop that allows you to save and apply specific tool settings, offering efficiency and flexibility in your work. These presets can be managed using various tools and panels within Photoshop:

1. Loading and Selecting Tool Presets:
- To select a tool preset, you can utilize the tool Preset selection pane within the options bar. This picker provides a pop-up panel from which you can choose the desired preset.
- Alternatively, you can access the Tool Presets window by going to "Window > Tool Presets." From this panel, you can browse and choose the default tool. That suits your needs.

2. Editing and Creating Presets:
- Tool presets are not only for selecting but also for editing and creating. You can customize and adjust the settings of existing presets to match your preferences.
- To create new tool presets, you can define the settings, save them, and add them to your library. These personalized presets can be accessed and reused for future projects.

3. Managing Presets with the Preset Manager:
- For more advanced management of your tool presets, the Preset Manager is a valuable resource. This instrument enables you to organize, import, export, and delete presets efficiently.

Create a tool presets

Use these procedures to make a gadget that was pre-programmed in Photoshop:

1. Select a Tool and Configure Settings:

- Begin by choosing a specific tool within Photoshop.

- Adjust and configure the settings for that tool Within the choices bar, configuring them according to your preferences.

2. **Access the Tool Preset Options**:
   - You have two options to access the tool preset options:
   - Press the Tool Preset menu item., typically located next to the tool on the choices bar's left side.
   - Alternatively, navigate to "Window > Tool Presets" to open the Tool Presets panel.

3. **Create the Tool Preset**:
   - Within the Tool Presets window, you can create the tool preset by taking one of the following actions:
   - Click The button labeled "Create New Tool Preset"
   - Click on "New Tool Preset" in the panel's menu.

4. **Name the Tool Preset**:
   - A dialog will appear, prompting you to provide a name for your newly created tool preset.
   - Enter a descriptive name that reflects the purpose or settings of the preset.

5. **Confirm and Save**:
   - After naming your Tool Preset: Choose the "OK" or "Save" button to save your configuration as a tool preset.

Change the list of tool presets

Use these procedures to change the Photoshop tool preset list:

1. **Access the Tool Presets Pop-Up Menu**:

- Click on the triangle icon under the Tool Presets pop-up panel to open the menu.

2. **Choose a Display Option**:
   - From the pop-up panel menu, choose from the following options. Options:
   - Display Every Tool Preset: This option displays all the currently loaded presets in the list.
   - Sort By Tool: Use this option to organize the presets based on the specific tool they are associated with.
   - Show Current Tool Presets: This choice filters and displays only the presets relevant to the tool that is currently in use. You can also enable the option for "Current Tool Only" within the Tool Presets pop-up panel to achieve the same result.
   - Simply Text, a Short List, or an Extended List: These options allow you to customize how the presets are presented within the pop-up panel, providing different views for your convenience.

How to open photos

Open File

The primary method to open files is through the "Open" command. It allows you to browse your computer's file system and select the image or record you wish to work on.

Another option is the "Open Recent" command, which provides quick access to recently accessed files. This feature is handy for swiftly revisiting and continuing work on recent projects.

Photoshop seamlessly integrates with various other Adobe applications such as Illustrator, Fresco, Lightroom, and Bridge. You can open files directly from these applications into Photoshop, streamlining your creative process.

When opening specific file types like camera raw and PDF, you may encounter dialog boxes where you can specify settings and options. These settings allow you to configure how the file is processed and presented in Photoshop, ensuring that it aligns with your project requirements.

Open a file with the use of the open command

To use Photoshop's "Open" command to open a file, take these steps:

1. **Access the "Open" Command**:

   - Click on "File" in the menu bar.

   - Select "Open" from the list that drops below.

2. **Choose the File**:
   - A file dialog box will open, allowing you to browse your computer and select the file you wish to open.
   - If the desired file is not immediately visible, you can select the option to display all files. This option may be found under "Files Of Type" (Windows) or "Enable" (Mac OS) in the pop-up menu.

3. **Open the File**:
   - Once you've chosen the file, click the "Open" button.
   - In some cases, a dialog box may appear, providing you with the opportunity to set format-specific options, which allow you to configure the file's properties according to your preferences.

Important Note: If you encounter a color profile warning message, you will be prompted to choose the use of color profiles. You can decide whether to use the embedded profile as the working space, convert the document color to the working space, or reverse the embedded profile, depending on your project's color management needs.

Open a recently used file.

To choose a file from the submenu and access recently opened files in Photoshop, take the following actions:

1. Click on "File" in the menu bar.

2. Choose "Open Recent" from the dropdown menu.

3. A submenu will appear, displaying a list of recently opened files.

4. Select the file you want to reopen from this submenu.

NB: In case you desire to control the number of files displayed in the "Open Recent" menu, you can adjust this setting in the File Handling preferences:

- For Windows, navigate to "Edit > Preferences > File Handling."

- For Mac OS, go to "Photoshop > Preferences > File Handling."

Make a specification of the file format in which the file should be opened

To open a file in Photoshop using a specific file format, take the following actions:

For Windows:

1. Click on "File" in the menu bar.
2. Choose "Open As" and select the file you wish to open.

3. From the "Open As" pop-up menu, select the desired format for the file.
4. Click "Open" to open the file with the specified format.

For macOS:

1. Click on "File" in the menu bar.
2. Choose "Open" and select "All Documents" from the "Show" pop-up menu.
3. Select the file you want to open.
4. From the "Format" pop-up menu, choose the desired file format for the file.
5. Click "Open" to open the file with the specified format.

Note: If the selected format doesn't match the file's true format, or if the file is damaged, it may not open successfully. In such cases, ensure that you've chosen the correct format or consider the possibility that the file might be corrupted.

Open PDF Files

Adobe Portable Document Format (PDF) is a highly adaptable file format that accommodates the representation of both vector and bitmap data. This format is equipped with advanced features for electronic document searching and navigation. PDF stands as the primary file format utilized by Adobe Illustrator and Adobe Acrobat.
PDF files can vary in complexity, with some containing single images and others comprising multiple pages and images. When you choose to open a PDF file in Photoshop, you gain the flexibility to select specific pages or images for opening and to define preferences for rasterization.

Moreover, you have the option to import PDF data into Photoshop through various means, such as the Place command, the Paste command, and the drag-and-drop feature. The imported page or image is positioned on a separate layer as a smart object, enabling further manipulation and integration into your Photoshop projects.

Please be aware that opening ordinary Adobe Photoshop PDF files requires the precise steps listed below. When dealing with Photoshop PDF files, there is no need to specify any preferences in the Dialog Box for Importing PDF.

This is the methodical procedure:

1. Take one of the following actions:

- For Photoshop: Go to the "File" menu, Select the file you wish to open by opening the dialog box. And click "Open."
- For Bridge: Choose "File" > "Open" after selecting the PDF file> "Adobe Photoshop."

For Both Photoshop and Bridge:

2. In the Open dialog box, locate and choose the specific file you intend to open, and then click the "Open" button.

3. Within the Import PDF dialog box, you will find the "Select" option. Depending on your requirements for importing elements from the PDF document, make a selection between "Pages" or "Images."

4. To designate the pages or images for opening, click on the respective thumbnails. If necessary select multiple pages or images, simply firmly press the Shift key. While clicking. The number of items you've selected will be indicated beneath the preview window.

5. To assign a name to the new document, enter the desired name in the provided "Name" text box. When you are importing multiple pages or images, each document will open with a base name, followed by a numerical identifier.

6. In the "Page Options" section, you can tailor the inclusion of the PDF file by selecting the "Crop To" option. There are several options available:

- **Bounding Box**: This option trims the record of the smallest rectangular area encompassing all text and graphics on the page. It effectively removes any unnecessary white space and elements located outside the Trim Box.

Here are the options available in the "Crop To" menu, each specifying a different area for cropping:

- **Media Box:** Resizes to resize to the original page size.
- **Crop Box:** Adjusts the PDF file's crop margins or clipping area.
- **Bleed Box:** Crops to the area specified in the PDF file to account for constraints relating to production, such as cutting, folding, and trimming.
- **Trim Box:** Trims the page to the designated region for the intended final size.
- **Art Box:** This feature crops the PDF file to the area that is selected so that the PDF data may be used in another program.

7. In the "Image Size" section, you can input values, if needed, for both the "Width" and "Height" parameters. Here's how to manage the aspect ratio and scaling:

- To maintain the aspect ratio of the pages while adjusting them to fit within the defined rectangle formed by the "Width" and "Height" values, check the "Constrain Proportions" option.
- If you prefer to scale the pages precisely to the specified "Width" and "Height" values, uncheck the "Constrain

Proportions" option. Be aware that there might be some distortion in the scaled pages.

When multiple pages are selected, the dimensions "Width" and "Height" text boxes will display the maximum width and height values among the selected pages. If "Constrain Proportions" is enabled and you do not modify the "Width" and "Height" values, all pages will be rendered at their original sizes. Altering these values will proportionately scale all the selected pages as they are rasterized.

8. Specify the following options under **Image Size**:

- **Resolution**: This establishes the resolution for the newly created document. For more information on pixel dimensions and printed image resolution, refer to the relevant section.
- **Mode**: This determines the color mode for the new document. Additional details on color modes can be found in the respective section.
- **Bit Depth**: This specifies the bit depth for the new document. To learn more about bit depth, please consult the corresponding section.

The ultimate pixel dimensions of the resulting document are determined by the "Width" and "Height" values, in conjunction with the "Resolution."

9. If you wish to suppress any color profile warnings, you can check the "Suppress Warning" option, and then proceed by clicking "OK."

Open an EPS File

Encapsulated PostScript, or EPS, is a popular file format used by graphic, illustration, and page-layout software programs because it is a flexible format that can handle bitmap and vector data with ease.

Adobe Illustrator is a key tool for expertly producing PostScript artwork.

When you access an EPS file featuring vector artwork, a transformative process occurs. The precisely defined lines and curves that constitute the vector art undergo a conversion, transitioning into the pixels and bits that form a bitmap image. This transition, referred to as rasterization, allows for the preservation of your intricate vector artwork in a bitmap format.

Should you wish to integrate your PostScript artwork into Adobe Photoshop, you have several convenient options at your disposal:

1. **Making Use of the Place Command:** This method enables you to import your PostScript artwork seamlessly into Photoshop.

2. **Leveraging the Paste Command:** By simply pasting your artwork into Photoshop, you Can swiftly incorporate your PostScript creations.

3. **Drag-and-Drop Feature**: For an intuitive and user-friendly experience, you can effortlessly drag and drop your PostScript artwork directly into Photoshop.

Use Photoshop to access your PostScript artwork by doing the following steps:

1. **Choose File > Open:** Initiate the process by navigating to the "File" menu and selecting "Open."

2. **Select the Desired File**: Locate the specific EPS file you intend to work with and select it. Confirm your selection by clicking "Open."

3. **Set Measurements, Clarity, and Mode:** Give your artwork the Measurements, Clarity, and Mode that you want it to have to make it fit your exact specifications. Choose the "Constrain Proportions" option to keep the height-to-width ratio at its original value.

Additionally, You might wish to choose "Anti-aliased" for edges that are smoother and free of artifacts.

Methods for Preserving Your Work

When it comes to preserving your Photoshop creations, you have a range of saving options and file formats at your disposal:

1. **PSD Format**: This is the default file type for Photoshop documents. It's your go-to format for retaining all the intricacies of your work, including layers and other crucial information. Photoshop is the intended application for opening PSD files allowing you to revisit and edit your project at a later time. However, if you intend to share your masterpiece you'll also need to store a duplicate for use with others in a more common file format, such as JPEG.

2. **Common File Formats**: If you're aiming for compatibility and easy sharing, you can opt for common files such as PNG and JPEG. These formats are ideal for collaboration since they can be viewed and edited on almost any computer or mobile device. Remember that these formats differ from PSD files in that are less suitable for ongoing editing, and they can't preserve the valuable layer information.

3. **Save for Web:** Planning to showcase your image on the internet, be it a blog or a website? Your greatest ally is the "Save for Web" option. It enables you to produce web-friendly photos ensuring quick and efficient downloading and seamless online viewing. "Save for Web" also comes equipped with a range of tools for web preparation, including image resizing options.

In the illustration below, you'll find A picture file can have three different formats: its original JPEG file, an altered PSD version, and a final JPEG version that has been downsized and optimized for the internet. Notice how the web version boasts significantly less space-consuming in comparison to the PSD and original versions, making it an ideal choice for online sharing and faster load times. Whether you're preserving your creative work, sharing it with others, or preparing it for the digital realm, Photoshop offers a spectrum of saving options to cater to your every need.

When harnessing the power of Photoshop's Save for the Online function, a few critical decisions must be made regarding the image you're preserving:

1. **File Format:** The Online Save tool provides a selection of web-safe file formats. For most photographic content, JPEG is the go-to choice. PNG-24 retains the image's full superiority, which makes it perfect for maintaining the highest fidelity, while PNG-8 is primarily suited for graphics and illustrations with a limited color palette. In most cases, the GIF and WBMP formats won't be necessary.

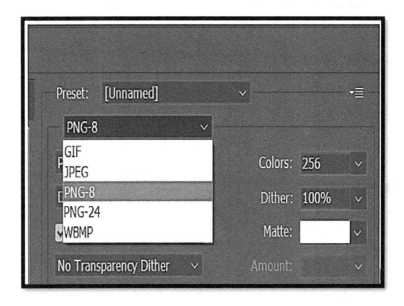

2. **Image Size:** The ability to Simply resize the picture. The dialog window labeled Save for Web is at your disposal. Reducing the image size simultaneously trims down the file size. However, when utilizing platforms such as Facebook or Tumblr, resizing may not be required, as these services often handle resizing automatically.

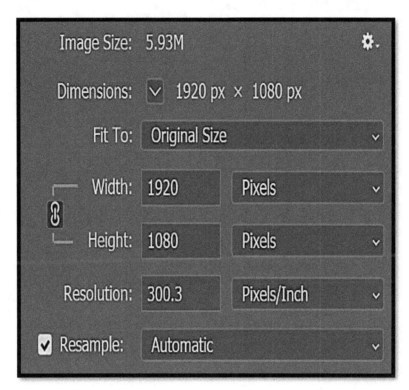

3. **Quality:** You can select from a range of quality options to alter the visual quality if you have opted for the JPEG format. By playing with different parameters, you may customize it to your requirements and determine the optimal balance between file size and image quality. Photoshop's Save for Online function gives you the power to make well-informed decisions about image optimization online, so your graphics are balanced, web-ready, and meet your rigorous standards.

Here's Your Guide to " Photoshop's "Save for Web" option:

1. **Access "Save for Web":** Start by selecting "File" > "Save for Web" from the Photoshop menu.

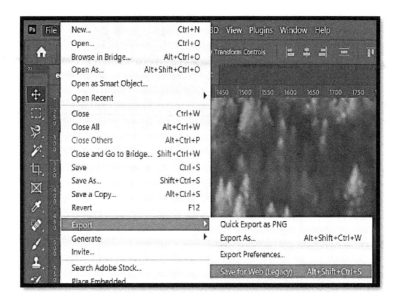

2. **Configure File Format and Level of Quality:** Once you've initiated "Save for Web," the dialog box will materialize. Here, you can fine-

tune your image by choosing the preferred quality level and file format.

3. **Resize the Image (if necessary):** Should you need to adjust the image size, simply input your preferred measurements found under "Image Size." The beauty of this feature is that when you modify the picture width and height will automatically adjust to maintain the original proportion of aspect.

4. **4. Employ the Up-Up View:** If you wish to contrast a glimpse of the updated image with the original, you can employ the "2-Up View." This is a convenient method to ensure that you haven't sacrificed excessively high quality from the original image. Take note of the file size displayed in each preview window's lower-left corner for reference.

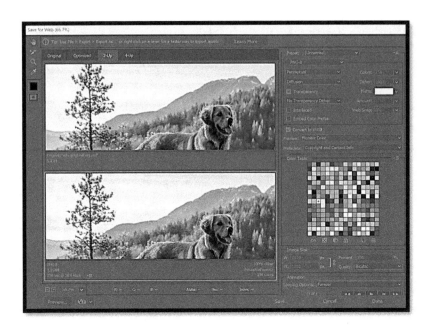

5. **Finalize the Save:** Click on "Save," and A fresh dialog window will appear to emerge. Here, you can specify the intended file name and select a file location. It's advisable to opt for a fresh file name to prevent any inadvertent overwriting of the original file.

Save

Saving your document is a fundamental and crucial action when working with any software, and it ensures that your current progress is preserved and any modifications you've made are securely stored. In this case, we'll explore the process of saving your document in the current format using the "File > Save" option.

1. **Preservation of Changes:** When you've invested time and effort into creating or editing a document, it's paramount to save your work to prevent any data loss. Selecting "File > Save" is your way of telling the software, in this case, the specific application you're using, that you want to keep the current version of your document with all the latest alterations.

2. **Document Format:** Every software application typically has a native or default file format where documents are created or edited. By choosing "File > Save," you are retaining your document in its existing format. This means that The text will be stored with the same file type and structure it had when you initially opened or created it.

3. **Version Control:** Saving in the current format also helps with version control. Each time you save, you create a snapshot of your document in its current state. If you make additional changes then save once more after that, you can access different versions of your document at various points in time. This can be incredibly useful If you would like to go back to a previous version or compare changes you've made over time.

4. **Safety and Security:** Saving your work is a safety net. It ensures that even if your software or device unexpectedly crashes or experiences technical issues, your latest progress is safe and can be

recovered. It provides a sense of security, knowing that your hard work won't go to waste due to unforeseen circumstances.

5. **Best Practices:** It's considered a best practice to save your document periodically, especially after significant edits or changes. This approach minimizes the risk of data loss and allows you to have multiple points in time to return to if needed.

Save As

Concerning saving your work in various formats, including PSD, JPEG, and PNG, the Save As command is your trusty tool. Here's a step-by-step guide on how to use it:

1. Open your image in Photoshop.

2. Navigate to the "File" menu, then select "Save As."

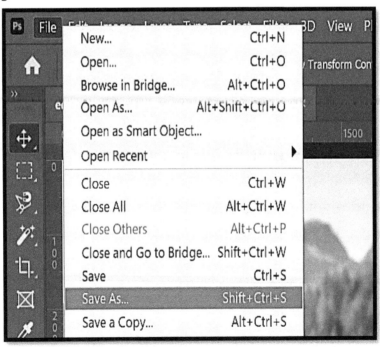

3. An interface window will pop up. Enter your preferred file name, and choose where you'd like to save the file. It's best to use a new

file name so you don't mistakenly overwrite your existing one.

4. Click on the "Format" menu within the dialog box, and choose the file format that you want. For instance, if you're saving the picture in JPEG format, make sure to pick that format. Note that when saving as a PSD file, you'll have the option to check the "Layers" box, but the majority of other formats won't provide this choice.

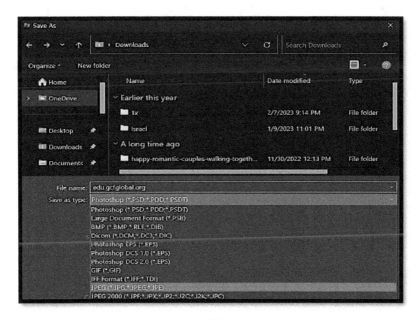

5. Once you've made your selections, hit the "Save" button.

6. Some formats, including TIFF and JPEG, may offer additional settings for you to adjust the quality level. After configuring these settings, Press "OK" to store the picture.

7. If your project has already been saved As a PSD file, you can easily save your work at any time by choosing "File" > "Save" or by using the keyboard shortcut Ctrl+S (or Command+S on a Mac). To avoid accidentally overwriting your original file, it is recommended to use the Save As command while dealing with other formats, such as JPEG.

Pro Tip: In some instances, you may find that not all format options are available when saving. To access a wider range of formats, make sure to enable the "Legacy 'Save as'" feature. You can do this by going to "Edit" > "Preferences" > "Ctrl + K" > "File handling," and then checking the box next to "Enable Legacy 'Save as'." Once you've done that, click "OK."

Save a copy

When you're working on a project in graphics or design software, such as Adobe Photoshop or Adobe Illustrator, you often possess the choice to create documents with multiple layers. Layers are incredibly useful for editing and organizing your content. However, there might be situations where you wish to make savings a flattened, single-layer version of your document, especially for sharing, printing, or using it in contexts where layer information is not needed. Here's a closer look at why and how you might want to save a file with layers as a flat file:

Why save a file with layers as a flat file:

1. **Simplicity:** A flat file is more straightforward to work with in certain scenarios, particularly when you don't need the complexity of individual layers. For instance, when you're sharing your design with someone who doesn't need access to or shouldn't modify the individual elements, a single-layer file is more user-friendly.

2. **File Size:** Flattening a document can reduce its file size. If your project has multiple layers with high-resolution content, keeping all those layers can result in a significantly larger file. Converting it to a flat file can make it more manageable, which is important when considering storage or upload limitations.

3. **Compatibility:** Some platforms or applications may not support layered files. For instance, social media platforms often require single-layered formats for profile pictures or cover photos. Creating a flat-file ensures compatibility in such cases.

How to save a file with layers as a flat file:

To create a flat file out of a layered document, you can follow these steps:

1. **Produce a New Edition:** Understand that saving a flat file doesn't overwrite your original layered document. Instead, you produce a New Edition. This is important because it preserves the original layered file for future editing or reference.

2. **Use the "Save a Copy" Option:** In your software application, navigate to the menu labeled "File," and select "Save a Copy." This option ensures that your original document remains intact.

3. **Select the Desired Format:** In the dialog window labeled "Save a Copy", you can choose the format you want for your flat file. Common options include JPEG and PNG, but this may vary depending on your software.

4. **Save the Flat File:** After you've chosen the format, click the "Save" or equivalent button, and your document will be saved as a flattened version in the format you chose.

This approach allows you to maintain both the original layered file, which retains all the editing capabilities, and the new flat file, which is ideal for sharing and specific use cases. So, whether you're creating a flattened version for a client, for printing, or for a platform that requires it, this method ensures that you possess the flexibility and control you need in your design projects.

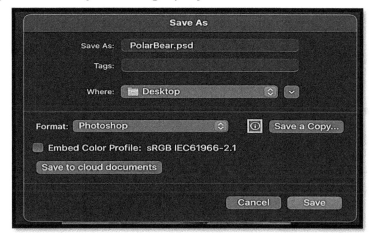

File Saving Properties

It's crucial to have the freedom to customize your saving choices to fit your unique requirements In terms of file storage. With the "Save As" and "Save a Copy" dialog boxes, you can adjust some properties depending on the kind of file you've both chosen file format and saving. A summary of these programmable file-saving attributes is provided below:

Alpha Channels: This option enables you to save or remove alpha channel information along with the image. Enabling this option ensures the preservation of alpha channels while disabling it will exclude alpha channels from the picture that was saved.

Layers: Every single layer in the image is retained if you choose to save layers. Depending on the chosen format, all visible layers are usually merged or flattened if this option is deactivated. This choice is particularly useful when you want to maintain the editability of layers in the saved file.

NB: This property provides you with the choice to save notes along with the image. Notes can be useful for adding annotations or explanations to the file for future reference or collaboration.

Spot Colors: Saving spot channel information is possible with this option. If disabled, spot colors are excluded from the picture that was saved. Spot colors are essential for specific printing processes or when you need precise color reproduction.

Color Management: You can create a color-managed document by utilizing options like " Utilize "ICC Profile" (Windows), "Proof Setup," or "Embed Color Profile" (Mac OS). These options are crucial for ensuring that the colors in your document are accurately represented in the saved file, particularly when working with professional printing or digital design.

Image Previews (Mac OS): These choices aren't accessible unless you've selected "Ask In the File Handling Preferences dialog box, choose "When Saving" for "Image Previews". It will be simpler to recognize your files if you save the thumbnail data for the file, which will show up in the Open dialog box.

Mac OS File Extension: You have the option to change the file extension format. Select "Use Lower Case" to make the extension lowercase and "Append" to add the format's extension to a filename. This can be useful for ensuring compatibility and consistency when sharing or managing files.

By understanding and using these customizable file-saving properties, you gain greater control over your files' characteristics, from layers and color management to additional information such as alpha channels and notes. It's an essential part of tailoring your files to meet the specific requirements of your projects and collaborators.

File saving preferences

You can adjust these settings to make sure your file-saving choices fit your workflow by doing the following steps:

For Windows Users:
1. Navigate to "Edit" and select "Preferences."
2. Choose "File Handling."

For macOS Users:
1. Click on "Photoshop" and choose "Preferences."
2. Opt for "File Handling."

Setting Options:

1. **Image Previews:** Determine how image previews are preserved. You can choose from three options:
   - To save files without a preview, select "Never Save".
   - To save files with certain previews, select "Always Save".
   - "Ask When Saving" to allocate previews to individual files. As mentioned in your Mac OS picture preview settings, if you're using macOS, you can choose one or more preview kinds.
2. **File Extension (Windows):** Personalized three-character file extensions that show a file's format. You have two choices:
   - When appending file extensions with uppercase letters, use "Upper Case."
   - "Use Lower Case" to attach lowercase letters to file extensions
3. **Attach File Extension (Mac OS):** File extensions are necessary if you plan to utilize or move files to a Windows computer. You can decide how extensions are appended to filenames:
   • Files lacking extensions are never saved using "Never".
   • Filenames are "Always" accompanied by a file extension.
   • You may add file extensions one file at a time by using "Ask When Saving". To add file extensions with lowercase letters, you may alternatively choose "Use Lower Case".
4. **Conserve in Original Folder:** By default, when saving, Photoshop will use the folder from which the images originated. If you prefer to default to the most recent stored folder, you can deselect this option.
5. **Store in Background**: Saving data in the background enables you to continue working in Photoshop even after initiating a Save command. This means you don't need to hold off till Photoshop completes saving the file, which can significantly improve your workflow efficiency.

6. Save Recovery Information Automatically: Photoshop can automatically store crash-recovery information at intervals you specify. In the event of a crash, this feature allows Photoshop to recover your work when you restart the application. It's a valuable safety net to protect your progress.

MACOS IMAGE PREVIEW OPTIONS

When using macOS, you have the flexibility to choose one or more preview types to optimize the saving of your files and reduce file size. Select only the previews that are relevant to your specific needs to ensure efficient file management.

1. **Icon:** This option utilizes the selected preview as the file's icon on your desktop. It illustrates a file that is easily recognizable at a glance.
2. **Full Size:** Selecting this option saves a 72ppi (pixels per inch) version of the file. This lower-resolution version is especially beneficial for applications that can only open low-resolution Photoshop images. For non-EPS files, this preview is in PICT format.
3. **Macintosh Thumbnail:** Enabling this option allows you to show the preview directly in the Open dialog box. It provides a quick visual reference for your files, facilitating the process of identifying and selecting the right document.
4. **Windows Thumbnail:** This option retains a sneak peek that is compatible with Windows systems. It ensures that your files can be easily displayed on Windows-based computers, enhancing cross-platform accessibility and compatibility.

Saving Large Documents

Photoshop offers extensive flexibility In terms of document dimensions and file formats, accommodating a wide range of creative projects. Here are the key details you need to know:

Document Dimensions: Photoshop can handle documents up to an impressive thirty thousand pixels in each direction This generous limit empowers you to work on intricate and high-resolution projects without constraints.

File Formats for Large Images: For images with dimensions exceeding thirty thousand pixels in each direction, Photoshop provides three specialized file formats to ensure compatibility and performance. It's worth noting that many other applications, including earlier versions of Photoshop like Photoshop CS, have limitations when dealing with pictures or files bigger than 2 GB surpassing thirty thousand pixels

1. Extended Document Format

- **Accommodates files of any size for documents.** Whether you're working on a project of standard proportions or something exceptionally large, the PSB format has you covered.
- **Preserves all Photoshop features.** Your document retains all the advanced capabilities and features of Photoshop, ensuring your creative freedom.
- **Note:** Some plug-in filters may become unavailable if your document exceeds thirty thousand pixels high or wide.
- **Compatibility:** PSB files are currently supported by Photoshop CS and subsequent versions.

2. Photoshop Raw:

- **Accommodates documents with any file size or pixel resolution:** Regardless of how large your project is, Photoshop Raw can accommodate it.
- **Flattened documents:** It's essential to be aware that Photoshop Raw is not compatible with layers. Big files stored in this format are automatically flattened.
- **Versatile Application:** This format is highly versatile, making it suitable for various purposes.

3. TIFF:

- **Files up to 4 GB in size are supported:** TIFF is a widely recognized and compatible format that can handle substantial file sizes.
- **Limitation:** Remember that TIFF files cannot be stored with sizes more than 4 GB.
- **Preferred Choice:** TIFF is often the preferred format for high-quality images due to its lossless compression and versatility.

Export Layers to Files

In Photoshop, you can efficiently export and save your layers as separate files, providing you with a range of format options such as PDF, Targa, TIFF, JPEG, PSD, and BMP. Each layer is automatically named during the saving process, but you also have the option to customize the naming convention to suit your needs. Here's how to navigate this process:

1. Access the Export Layers To Files Option:

- Start by selecting "File" > "Export" > "Export Layers to Files."

2. Define the Export Destination:

- Within the Dialog Box for Exporting Layers to Files, beneath the "Destination" section, click "Browse" to designate a destination folder for the exported files. These files are automatically stored in the same location as the original file.

3. Specify a Common File Name Prefix:

- To create a consistent naming convention for your exported files, enter a name in the "File Name Prefix" text field. This common prefix will be used for all the individual files, with unique identifiers appended as needed.

4. Control Layer Selection:

- If you only wish to export layers that are currently visible Inside the Layers panel, activate Using "Visible Layers Only". This is a practical choice if you don't want every single layer to be exported. You can manage layer visibility by toggling the visibility icon for each layer.

5. Choose the File Format:

- Through the menu item "File Type", select the file format that best suits your needs. Make any necessary format-specific adjustments or settings.

6. Include ICC Profile (for Color-Managed Workflows):

- If you're working in a color-managed environment and want to ensure consistent color reproduction, Choose "Include ICC Profile" from the menu. This embeds the export file's working area profile, a critical step in maintaining color accuracy.

7. Execute the Export Process:

- Once you've configured your export settings, click "Run" to initiate the export. Photoshop will process your layers and save them as distinct files in the designated destination folder.

This efficient process gives you the ability to easily export and save your layers as distinct files, streamlining your workflow and ensuring that your creative assets are organized and readily accessible in your preferred file formats.

What exactly is meant by Adobe Camera Raw?

Adobe Camera Raw

Adobe Camera Raw, a powerful software plug-in, seamlessly integrates with Adobe After Effects and Adobe Photoshop. It also adds valuable functionality to Adobe Bridge, enriching the capabilities of these applications by enabling them to import and manipulate camera raw files. What's more, Camera Raw extends its prowess to encompass the processing of JPEG and TIFF files, expanding its versatility.

Noteworthy Specifications: Camera Raw boasts impressive capabilities, supporting images with dimensions up to 65,000 pixels in length or width and accommodating files with a resolution of up to 512 megapixels. It's important to observe that when you open CMYK images with Camera Raw, they are automatically converted to RGB color space, aligning them with the application's color standards. For a comprehensive list of cameras supported by Camera Raw, you can refer to the Digital Camera Raw file support.

Intuitive Integration: To access Camera Raw via Adobe Bridge, you must have Adobe Photoshop or Adobe after Effects installed. This allows you to open files in the Camera Raw dialog box directly from Adobe Bridge. Even if you do not have Photoshop or After Effects installed, you can still preview images and access their metadata in Adobe Bridge. Furthermore, if another application is associated with the image file type, you can seamlessly open the file in that specific application from within Adobe Bridge.

Streamlined Workflow in Adobe Bridge: Within Adobe Bridge, you have the convenience of applying, copying, and clearing image settings. You can also preview Camera Raw files and access their metadata without the need to open them in the Camera Raw dialog box. The preview displayed in Adobe Bridge is a JPEG image generated based on the current image settings. It's worth noting that this preview is not the raw camera data itself, which would appear as a very dark grayscale image. A caution icon appears during the generation of the preview in the Camera Raw dialog box.

Customization and Presets: Camera Raw provides the flexibility to modify default settings for a specific camera model. Additionally, you may customize defaults for certain ISO levels or even for specific cameras that can be identified by their serial numbers. Additionally, you may modify and store picture parameters as presets. Which can be readily applied to other images as needed.

Preservation of Original Data: When using the original camera raw data is preserved while making changes to an image, such as cropping and straightening. The changes are either contained in a sidecar XMP file (a related metadata file that is attached to the camera raw file) or safely kept in the Camera Raw database as metadata embedded in the picture file. See the documentation for specific details on where Camera Raw settings are kept.

Seamless Transition to Photoshop: Following your processing and editing An identifying symbol appears in the picture thumbnail of a camera raw file created with the Camera Raw plug-in. Within Adobe Bridge, signifying its successful handling.

Flexible Export Options: When you open a camera raw file in Photoshop, you may choose to save the picture in PSD, JPEG, TIFF, Cineon, Photoshop Raw, PNG, or PBM, among other formats. You can save processed files in Photoshop (PSD), JPEG, TIFF, or Digital Negative (DNG) formats while using the Camera Raw dialog box in Photoshop.

Process images with Camera Raw

Adobe Camera Raw is a robust tool for working with camera raw files, enabling you to fine-tune and enhance your images. To make the most of this resource, follow these steps to ensure that your workflow is efficient and well-organized:

1. Transfer and Organize:
- Begin by copying the raw information from your camera to your computer's hard disk. This step is essential for proper organization, and it sets the stage for any further adjustments you wish to make. Optionally, you can convert your raw files to Digital Negative (DNG) format for added compatibility.

2. Use Adobe Bridge:
- To easily move your camera raw data from your memory card, use Adobe Bridge's "Get Photos From Camera" command. This procedure organizes your files automatically, gives them appropriate titles, and gets them ready for your creative projects.

3. Open in Camera Raw:
- Open your image files in Camera Raw. You may do this from Adobe Bridge, After Effects, Photoshop, or other programs. Moreover, JPEG and TIFF files may be opened straight from Adobe Bridge with Camera Raw.

4. Fine-Tune Color:

- Modify the color as needed, taking into account saturation, tone, and white balance. Most modifications may be made using the controls on the Basic page; other tabs offer more fine-tuning possibilities. If you'd like, you may select the "Auto" button on the Basic tab to let Camera Raw analyze your photo and make approximative tone changes.

5. Further Adjustments and Corrections:

- Use the many tools and settings in the Camera Raw dialog box to carry out further operations including noise reduction, retouching, sharpening images, and correcting lens defects.

6. Optional Presets and Default Settings:

- Save your settings as a preset for later use if you want to make the same alterations to several photographs. As an alternative, you may store your modifications as the factory defaults for a particular camera model, ISO, or camera parameter. This guarantees that any photos that satisfy the given criteria will automatically be assigned these default settings.

7. Workflow Options for Photoshop:

- To ensure a smooth integration between Camera Raw and Photoshop, set up the workflow settings to specify how Camera Raw photographs are saved and how Photoshop should open them. In the Camera Raw dialog box, these options are accessible by clicking the link located beneath the picture preview.

8. Completing Your Camera Raw Workflow

Once you've made the desired changes to the raw camera footage, it's time to wrap up your workflow by choosing the appropriate action for your image. Here are the available options:

1. Save the Image:

- The raw camera footage file can be saved once the modifications have been applied. As an alternative, you can save the modified picture in an alternative format. This is especially helpful if you want to keep the adjustments in place and are happy with them. Note that you can save the files using the last set of save choices and suppress the Camera Raw Save choices dialog box by hitting Alt (Windows) or Option (Mac OS). See the manual for further information on how to save a camera raw image in a different format.

2. Open in Photoshop or After Effects:

- Images from the camera raw files may be opened immediately in Photoshop or After Effects, together with the applied Camera Raw parameters. It is still the raw picture from the original camera. You may open the raw file as a Smart Object in Photoshop by holding down the Shift key when selecting "Open Image." As a result, by double-clicking the Smart Object layer that contains the raw file, you may always tweak the Camera Raw settings.

3. Finalize and Store Settings:

- Once your Camera Raw session is over, choose "Done". With this operation, the Camera Raw dialog box is closed and your file settings are saved as a DNG file, a sidecar XMP file, or the camera raw database file. It guarantees that your modifications are kept for future use.

4. Cancel Adjustments:

- To undo the changes you made in the Camera Raw dialog box, select "Cancel." Choosing this option restores the picture to its initial condition and undoes all alterations.

Camera Raw plug-in overview

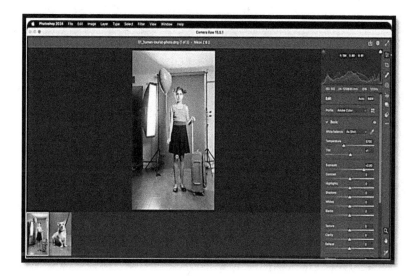

Panels

In your editing journey, the Edit panels serve as powerful tools to fine-tune your images and achieve the desired results. Here's a quick manual explaining how to access and use these panels in Adobe Bridge:

Accessing the Edit Panels:

- To access the Edit panels, navigate to the right portion of the dialog box. These panels provide you with a wide array of adjustment options to enhance your images.

Using Edit Panels in Adobe Bridge:

- For Adobe Bridge users, these options can also be found under Edit" > "Develop Configurations. This accessibility ensures that you can make your adjustments seamlessly.

Customizing Your Workspace:

- The Edit panels can be opened or collapsed according to your specific needs. Once you've made adjustments within a panel, you have the option to conceal the preview's modifications made in that panel by long-pressing the eye icon. Additionally, you can The Profile drop-down menu allows you to choose a profile. When you've completed your desired adjustments, simply click "Done" to proceed.

A Closer Look at Edit Panels:

1. **Basic:** Use the user-friendly sliders to adjust White Balance, Temperature, Tint, Exposure, Highlights, Shadows, and other aspects of your image.
2. **Curve:** Use curves to get exact control over the tonal scale. The Red, Green, and Blue channels' curves as well as the Parametric Curve and Point Curve are available options.
3. **Detail:** Easily manipulate the image sharpness, noise reduction, and color noise reduction using the included sliders.
4. **Color Mixer:** Explore adjustments to hues, saturation, and luminance (HSL) or make color corrections within your image.
5. **Color Grading**: Use the color wheels to achieve complex hue alterations in the Shadows, Midtones, and Highlights. Perfect the way these colors flow together and are balanced.
6. **Optics:** Fix typical optical problems including distortion, vignetting, and chromatic aberration. You may also use the

Defringe function to highlight and adjust any purple or green tones in your picture.

7. **Geometry:** Make flexible changes to vantage points and elevations. You can easily eliminate any white borders that may emerge after performing Geometry modifications by selecting the "Constrain crop" option.

8. **Effects:** Add artistic elements to your image, whether it's grain for texture or a vignette to draw attention, using the provided sliders.

9. **Calibration:** Adjust the Shadows, Red Primary, Green Primary, and Blue Primary settings after choosing your preferred Process Version from the Process drop-down box.

Crop and Adjust Composition

- Adjust the angle and aspect ratio to get the best possible composition for your photos. Easily flip and rotate your photos to improve their visual impact.

Spotless Image Enhancement

- Effortlessly heal or replicate particular regions within your image, ensuring a flawless and spotless final result.

Targeted Brush Edits

- Take precise control of your editing with the Adjustment Brush tool, allowing you to make detailed changes to particular regions of your photo.

Gradual Control

- The Graduated Filter offers you the power to create selections Using parallel lines. Modify several parameters according to the location you have chosen, enabling improvements.

Radiant Effects

- With the Radial Filter, craft selections using an ellipse, and fine-tune settings based on your chosen areas to create stunning effects and focal points.

Red Eye Correction
- Bid farewell to erythema or ocular irritation in your images effortlessly. Adjust the pupil size or apply a darkening effect for a more natural look.

Snapshot Your Progress
- Create and preserve various altered copies of your photo, allowing you to experiment without losing your original work.

Effortless Preset Usage
- Discover an array of superior picture presets, various skin tones, cinematic effects, travel vibes, vintage aesthetics, and more. In addition, your user presets are readily accessible. A simple linger over an already-set provides a preview, and a single click applies it to your image.

Explore Presets

Unlock a world of creative potential with our premium presets, thoughtfully crafted for a range of purposes. Dive into a selection of presets curated for portraits, catering to various skin tones. Embrace cinematic moods, capture the essence of travel, or infuse a touch of vintage charm into your images. Your user presets are also at your fingertips. Effortlessly preview each preset by hovering over it and bringing your chosen style to life with a simple click.

Image Preview

The image on the left showcases a preview of your applied edits. Easily switch between " By selecting the symbol in the lower-right corner, you can see the "Before" and "After" perspectives. Allowing you to see the transformation at a glance. Additionally, you have the flexibility to toggle between settings while simultaneously comparing the image with and without edits. To focus on specific adjustments, you can temporarily conceal modifications made to a panel by long-pressing the eye icon of that panel, granting you full control over your editing process.

Image Filmstrip

The images you launch in Raw Camera are neatly showcased in the filmstrip, located just below the preview area. This filmstrip provides easy access to all your images, allowing for efficient browsing and selection.

Customization at Your Fingertips

You have the freedom to enhance your viewing experience. Hide the filmstrip if you prefer a clutter-free workspace. Arrange your images with the options to sort depending on the file name, star rating, capture date, and Color Label. If you're searching for specific photos, the Filter icon permits the use of filters for a streamlined selection process.

Enhanced Portraiture Workflow

For portrait work and similar tasks, you can optimize your workspace by relocating the filmstrip to the panel on the left. To make this adjustment, simply Control-click (macOS) or Right-click (Windows) on the filmstrip, then choose "Filmstrip Orientation." " followed by "Vertical." This orientation is particularly valuable when focusing on portrait editing, providing a more intuitive and organized workspace.

Additional Navigation Options

Explore further control options to enhance your editing experience:

Zoom Tool:

- The Zoom tool, which can be found at the bottom of the right panel, makes it simple to change your view. As needed, adjust the zoom level of the preview image. You may quickly get back to the "Fit in View" option by double-clicking the Zoom symbol. You may also adjust the zoom level with the Zoom level option, which is located beneath the filmstrip and has a 100% default setting.

Hand Tool:

- Use the Hand tool to precisely navigate across your zoomed-in image. You can navigate and investigate different sections of the preview image. Holding down the spacebar allows you to quickly move from one tool to the Hand tool while still using the other. To smoothly resize the sample picture to fit the window, double-click the Hand tool.

What are Raw Images?

Within the field of photography, RAW photographs are essential. These files contain raw, uncompressed image data that are practical as a blank canvas to record a wide range of features seen via the lens. The RAW format, in contrast to other raster file types, excels at maintaining the highest degree of detail, providing photographers with a canvas for significant manipulation, compression, and eventual conversion into other formats.

Why should Camera Raw be used to edit pictures?

Any layer or RAW file in Photoshop can be quickly edited using Adobe Camera Raw, a strong and user-friendly built-in plugin. With a camera raw, you can expertly edit your images without causing any damage, improving aspects like hues, exposure, and other factors. The reasons Camera Raw is used for editing are:

1. Simplified Color and Exposure Corrections, Minus Layers

Photoshop makes it challenging to make simple photo alterations; even simple edits can need several complex processes. Now for the game-changing Camera Raw. Without the hassle of layers, you can easily adjust your photos here. Bid farewell to complex layer management and welcome Camera Raw's intuitive sliders for your tweaks. When you access a raw file in Photoshop, Camera Raw opens automatically. There's no need for complicated procedures—just go to "File" > "Open," choose the files you want, and see how much easier editing can be.

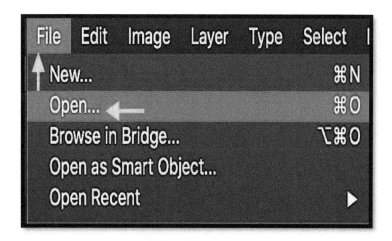

But raw data isn't the only thing that Camera Raw can do. It expands to encompass files in the TIFF or JPEG formats. To accomplish this, just pick "Filter" > "Camera Raw Filter," which will reveal the pre-existing layer you have chosen when the Camera Raw interface opens. On Macs, Shift + Command + A is a useful shortcut for rapid access, whereas on PCs, Shift + Control + A swiftly expands your editing options.

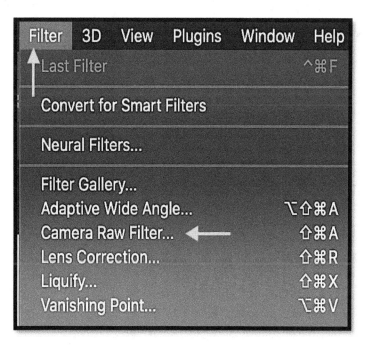

When you start editing in Camera Raw, make sure the Edit icon (at the top of the left toolbar) is chosen.

This interface contains a plethora of editing tools just waiting for your creative input. For instance, the Basic panel makes it simple to adjust exposure, but the Color Mixer or Color Grading sections are where color improvements go. You may adjust temperature changes with precision with the Basic Panel, giving you complete control over the appearance of your image.

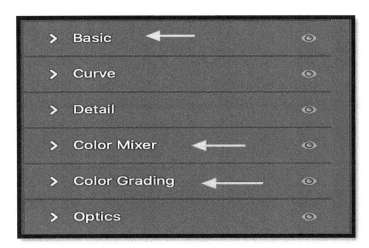

The tools in Camera Raw are designed to be as easy to use as feasible. It's simple to increase or reduce exposure by sliding the bar up or down. In a similar vein, adjusting the Hue, Saturation, and Luminance (HSL) of various colors is a snap when utilizing basic sliders.

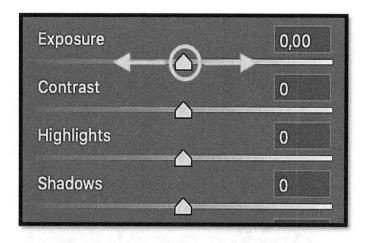

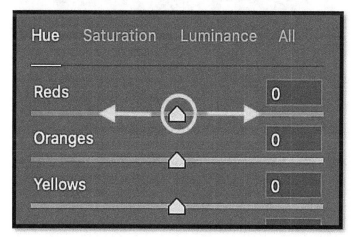

2. Simplified Multiple Editing

Although batch editing with Photoshop is technically possible, the procedure might be too complicated and demand a significant amount of steps. Camera Raw makes batch editing much more efficient by streamlining and simplifying the process.

Open your files for editing by selecting the RAW images you wish to work on under "File" > "Open" if you want to edit many photographs at once. You may choose a lot of photographs rapidly by holding down "Command" on a Mac or "Control" on a PC while you pick the right pictures.

Simply click on the chosen photographs in the Camera Raw box that appears by holding down the "Command" or "Control" keys on a Mac or PC to mark all the photos you wish to edit. Once the photographs have been chosen, a gray outline will appear around them, signifying that they are now ready for editing.

Then, whatever changes You arrive at the center of the image you're executing will automatically apply to all the other images you've chosen. The previews at the bottom of the interface will dynamically adjust to reflect the modifications you're making, making this real-time synchronization easy to see.

Please be informed that any changes you make will only impact the image you are now editing if you choose not to choose the photos.

3. Exclusive Use of Special Tools

Explore Camera Raw to find a variety of tweaks that are hard to come by in other Photoshop sections. Although Photoshop enables you to adjust the colors of an image, there isn't a specific tool for color grading. This also holds for often utilized improvements such as texture and clarity tweaks.

You may access these specialist tools within Camera Raw, which is an independent workspace from the Photoshop main workspace. The advantages of using Camera Raw for editing are enhanced by the availability of options beyond traditional adjustment layers.

4. Easy-to-use Selective Modifications

Photoshop has amazing powers, but its large toolbox and features, especially for beginners, can be daunting. Adjusting layers and layer masks are two confusing ideas for people who are not familiar with picture editing.

For inexperienced photographers, comprehending the subtleties of layer manipulation can be an overwhelming undertaking. Camera Raw's selective modification capabilities offer a far more convenient option in these situations. These include the radial filter, the graded filter, and the adjusting brush.

Just open your shot in Camera Raw and go to the right-hand toolbar to make use of these capabilities. The adjustment brush tool allows you to selectively apply paint over certain areas of the image and make adjustments there. Open this tool by clicking the brush symbol.

The Size bar, which appears as a floating circle on your image, makes it simple to adjust the brush size. Click the arrow next to the Size setting to bring up dropdown options for feathering, flow, and density.

These options provide you with fine-grained control over the properties of your brush.

Simply move your mouse over your image to see a circle that represents the brush size to adjust the brush size. Its size may be adjusted using the Size bar. To fine-tune the brush's feathering, flow, and density, click the arrow next to the Size option to see drop-down selections.

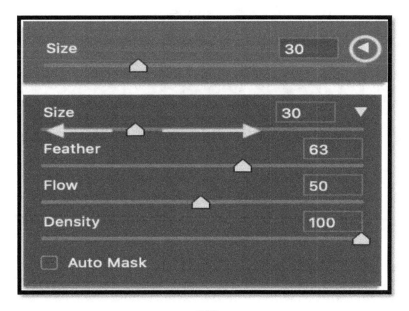

Below these options, you'll find a variety of modifications that you can apply to the edits you've chosen.

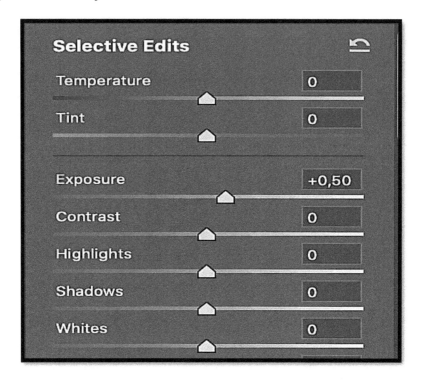

Just choose the eraser tool, then resize its size to your desired level to undo the spot brush modifications.

Moving on, the graded filter works by modifying your shot in a gradient style. Click the correct icon to activate this tool, then Drag and drop the filter. To the desired location inside your image. Engaging with the dashed lines in green or red makes it simple to change the filter's rotation and width.

Conveniently, the adjustment options are situated next to the brush. Additionally, by only pressing the eraser icon, you may remove any portion of the filter.

Like the other two selective adjustment tools, the radial filter operates similarly. You can drag the filter onto your image and sculpt it into the appropriate radial shape by clicking the corresponding icon. You have the choice to switch between resizing the filter as you go to suit your tastes.

Using the feather option, you may change the degree of feathering for a more understated look by increasing or lowering it as necessary.

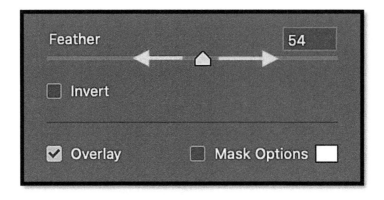

5. Enables Simple Picture Editing Quickly

Even though Photoshop is a flexible program with complex picture editing capabilities, basic photo editing can take a great deal of time. Camera Raw, on the other hand, has an easy-to-use interface. It tidily gathers all the necessary adjustments in one location, each with simple functionality and clear labeling. The editing procedure is further expedited by the effective batch-editing capability. All in all, this means that using Camera Raw to alter your pictures is smooth and easy, especially In terms of undoing changes, which takes us to our next point.

6. Non-destructive picture editing is made easier with Camera Raw

Which makes it simple to remove or reverse any changes you've made. It's easier to determine what has to be reversed or identify particular modifications when you're not working with numerous layers. Click on the ellipsis-shaped bottom icon on the right to return your image to its initial configuration and undo all adjustments.

Afterward, select "Reset to Default."

Alternatively, It is possible to double-click the slider to make a precise modification and return it to its initial settings. To reverse the most recent edit you made, use the keyboard shortcuts On a Mac, use Command + Z; on a PC, use Control + Z.

File Formats and Camera Raw

Raw File Extensions

RAW files enable photographers to capture nearly every detail they see via their viewfinder because they contain unedited and uncompressed image data. Out of all raster file types, RAW files hold the most detail, which photographers can then alter, reduce, and convert into other formats.

For Windows:
1. Close all Adobe applications.
2. Unzip the downloaded .zip file by double-clicking on it. Windows may automatically extract the contents.
3. Double-click the resulting .exe file to initiate the installer.
4. Observe the guidelines displayed on the screen.
5. Restart your Adobe applications.

For macOS:
1. Close all Adobe applications.
2. Get the file that was downloaded. To unzip the.zip file if you are using Camera Raw 10.5: double-click it.
3. To start the installer, double-click the. Pkg file.
4. Observe the guidelines displayed on the screen.
5. Restart your Adobe applications.

Launching Photoshop's Camera Raw Format

The "Open" dialog box will appear when you choose "File| Open⁺" from the Menu Bar to open a locally saved camera raw image in Photoshop for editing. Next, navigate to and choose the camera raw file to open for processing using this dialog box. The camera raw image will then open in Photoshop's "Camera Raw" dialog box when you click the "Open" button in the "Open" dialog box.

Save a camera raw image in another format.

You have the option to save camera raw files in the Camera Raw dialog box in various formats, including PSD, TIFF, JPEG, or DNG. When using the Save Image command within the Camera Raw dialog box, files are queued for processing and saving. This is particularly handy when processing multiple files in the Camera Raw dialog box and saving them in the same format.

Here's how to store camera raw files, step-by-step:

1. Firstly, in the Camera Raw dialog box locate and Select "Save Image" from the menu in the lower-left corner.

NB: On Windows, Alt-click; on Mac OS, Option-click Save to skip the Camera Raw Save Options dialog box when saving a file.

2. Choose the following choices from the Save choices dialog box:

- Destination: To save the file, select the desired place by clicking the Select Folder button and browsing there.

- File Naming: Organize image files by defining the filename according to a standard that includes details like the date and the serial number of the camera.

- Format: The Format option allows you to select a file format:

- Digital Negative (DNG): maintains a copy of the DNG-formatted raw camera file.

- JPEG: maintains JPEG copies of the camera's raw data with the ability to modify compression for both file size and image quality.

- TIFF: preserves duplicates of the unprocessed camera data in TIFF format, with the choices of zero, LZW, or ZIP compression.

- Photoshop: preserves clipped pixel data and saves copies of the camera raw files in PSD format.

3. Click Save to complete the process.

Compatibility

Indicates the versions of Camera Raw and Lightroom capable of reading the file.

Indicate if you would prefer DNG 1.1 or DNG 1.3 compatibility if you choose Custom. Lossless compression is used by default in the conversion process to ensure no data loss even during file size reduction. If you choose Linear (Demosaiced), the image data is stored in an interpolated format that may be read by other applications without the need for a profile for the digital camera used to take the picture.

JPEG Preview

Incorporates a JPEG preview within the DNG file. You can choose the preview size if you want to include a JPEG preview. When external apps provide JPEG previews, users may examine the contents of the DNG file without having to access the raw camera data.

Embed Original Raw File

Preserves the original raw picture data from the camera within the DNG file.

CHAPTER FOUR

WHAT TO KNOW ABOUT PIXEL ART

Pixel art is a type of digital art where the composition is made up of individual pixels. It is influenced by the low resolution and color depth of early video games and computer graphics. It is distinguished by its sharp edges, straightforward shapes, and pixel-perfect details.

Start Drawing with Pixel

Creating pixel art in Photoshop is easy after you set up a canvas specifically for creating pixelated images.

1. Start a fresh canvas.
2. Make a grid, but use pixels instead of inches.
3. Subdivisions should equal one.
4. Change the Nearest Neighbor (keeping sharp edges) picture interpolation option.
5. Employ the Pencil tool. To keep your lines sharp and distinct.

Introduction to Photoshop's pencil tool

Photoshop's Pencil Tool is a strong tool that lets you draw lines and create designs with distinct edges. Adobe Inc. created Photoshop, a well-known raster image editor that is utilized extensively in a variety of creative and design sectors, for Mac OS and Windows. It offers a multitude of functions and is utilized by specialists as well as people from diverse backgrounds.

Photoshop may be used to compose raster pictures by using many layers, alpha compositing, mask support, and compatibility with several color models such as RGB, CMYK, spot color, duotone, and CIELAB.

The Pencil Tool can be found in Photoshop's toolbar on the left. Users can activate it from there, allowing their creative ideas to come to life on the canvas. This virtual pencil offers options to customize color, opacity intensity, pencil diameter, and more. It offers many ways to improve the visual appeal of your work, enabling the creation of unique artwork with a hand-drawn or human touch, adding a distinct and personal element to your designs.

How to Use the Pencil Tool in Adobe Photoshop?

The Pencil Tool is a versatile tool in Adobe Photoshop that allows for precise and controlled drawing. To effectively use the Pencil Tool, follow these steps:

1. **Open the Pencil Tool:** The Tools panel contains the Pencil Tool. All you have to do is pick the Pencil Tool from the panel to activate it. To swiftly switch to the Pencil Tool, you may also hit Shift + B.
2. **Adjust Brush Tip Size**: The Pencil Tool's brush tip size is set to 1 pixel by default. Click the thumbnail or the arrow in the Brush Preset Picker option from the Options Bar to change the brush tip size.

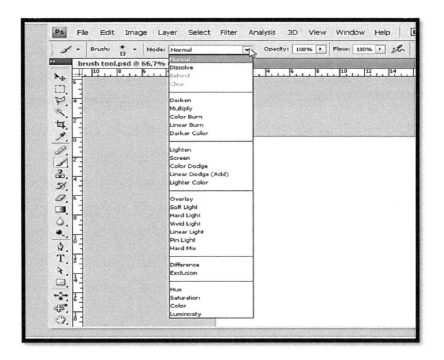

3. **Choose Blend Modes:** In the Mode Menu, you can select different modes for the Pencil Tool, such as Blend or other modes apart from Normal. Blend Modes enable colors to blend using various techniques. You can control the mode and opacity of the Pencil Tool in the Layers Panel on the drawing layer, allowing for flexibility and editing options.

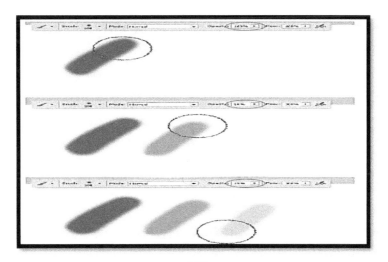

4. **Control Opacity:** The Pencil Tool's opacity may be changed by putting the required opacity percentage into the text box or by utilizing the opacity slider in the Layers Panel. It is helpful to utilize the opacity slider to partially or fully reveal the backdrop.

5. **Differentiating Pencil Tool and Brush Tool:** While there are many parameters that the Pencil Tool and Brush Tool have in common, one important difference is that the Pencil Tool's edges are harder than the Brush Tool's, which are softer and smoother. It is also possible to use the Pencil Tool as an eraser.

6. **Drawing Freehand Lines**: The Pencil Tool is useful for a variety of design and illustration projects since it makes it possible to create freehand lines precisely.

7. **Creating Straight Lines:** Click at the beginning point, let go of the mouse button, and then press Shift while clicking at the finishing point to draw a straight line between the two places. The two locations are connected by a straight line as a consequence.

8. **Foreground Color Change:** The foreground color is changed to the selected point's hue by clicking anywhere on the artboard and pressing the Alt key (Option key on a Mac). Its function allows for rapid color sampling.

9. **Keyboard Shortcuts:** Photoshop provides useful keyboard shortcuts that let you work more efficiently. As an example, the Move Tool is activated by pressing the V key, and the previously selected tool is returned when the key is released. By removing the need to browse to the Tools panel, this time-saving shortcut increases productivity.

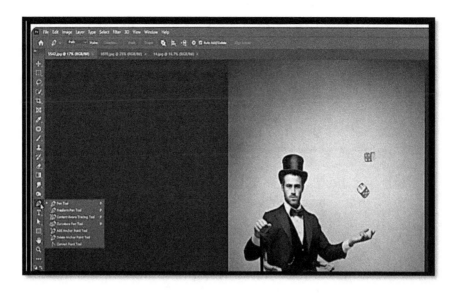

Steps to use the pencil tool

The Pencil Tool in Photoshop is an easy tool to use. This is a comprehensive guide on how to maximize the Pencil Tool's potential.

Step 1: Start a new document in Photoshop.

- Open Photoshop and create a new file to get started. To do this, navigate to "File" and select "New Document".

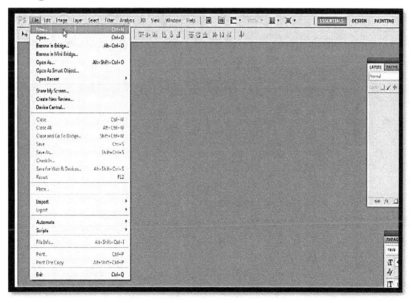

Step 2. Configure Document Settings.

- Follow these steps to modify the parameters for your newly created document. According to the specifications for your project, this entails defining the size, resolution, color mode, and other pertinent details.

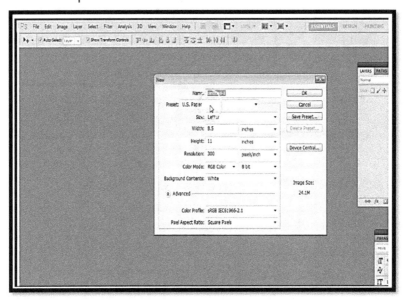

Step 3: Click the Toolbar and choose Tools.

- To utilize the Pencil Tool, go to the "Windows" menu and choose "Tools." To enable the toolbar if you can't find it, take the following actions.

Step 4: From the Toolbar, Make use of the Pencil Tool.

Find the Pencil Tool and Click on the toolbar.

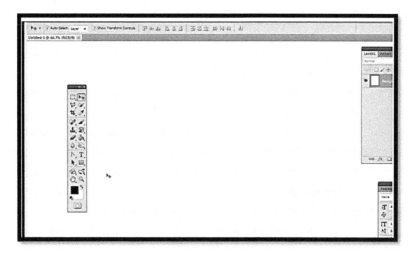

Step 5: Experiment with the Pencil Tool.

- Try sketching or drawing on the canvas while using the Pencil Tool chosen to get a sense of how it functions.

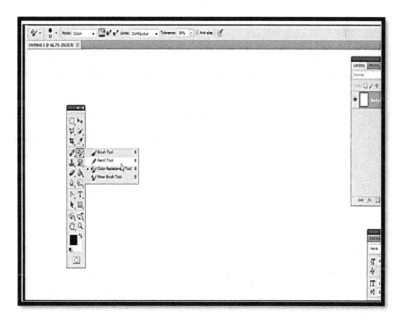

Step 6: In the Brush Preset Panel, adjust the brush's size and shape.

- Access the Panel for Brush Presets. Modify the brush's size and shape that the Pencil Tool uses. You can adjust your brush in this way to draw more precisely.

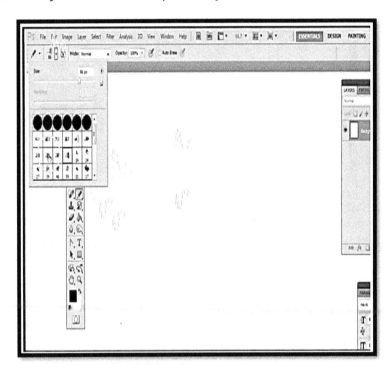

Step 7: Utilize the Pencil tool with a variety of brush styles.
- Play around with various brush techniques. To create a range of effects using the Pencil Tool. This provides flexibility in your drawing and design work.

Draw straight-line segments

Drawing straight line segments with the standard Pen tool in Photoshop involves creating a path consisting of straight line segments connected by corner points. Here's how you can do it:

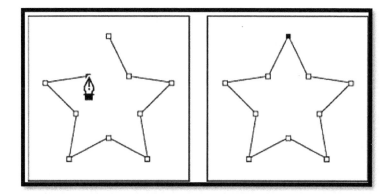

1. Click the Toolbar's Pen tool.
2. Click to establish the initial anchor point after positioning the Pen tool at the starting place where you want the straight section to begin (do not drag).

NB: You won't be able to see the initial segment you draw until you click on another anchor point. If you see direction lines, it indicates that you may have inadvertently moved the Pen tool. If so, select Edit > Undo, and then click once more.

3. Press the button once again to conclude the straight portion. Alternatively, you may Shift-click to limit the segment's angle to multiples of 45°.
4. Click again to set the anchor points for more straight segments.

The last anchor point you add will always show as chosen, looking like a solid square. As you add more anchor points, previously established anchor points become hollow and deselected.

To complete the path, you have two options:

- Place the Pen tool over the first (hollow) anchor point to close the route. A little circle appears next to the Pen tool cursor when it is positioned appropriately. Drag or click to end the route.

- You can Ctrl-click (Windows) or Command-click (Mac OS) anywhere away from any item to leave the path open. If you want to leave the path open, you may alternatively use a different tool.

Draw curves with the pen tool.

When using Photoshop's Pen tool to create curves, you must add anchor points at the locations where the curve's direction changes and modify the direction lines to give the curve shape. It is advisable to use as few anchor points as possible when drawing smooth curves since this improves display and printing performance and makes curves easier to alter. These are the instructions for using the Pen tool to create curves:

1. Go to the toolbar and select the Pen tool.
2. Holding down the mouse button, position the Pen tool where you want the curve to start. When the Pen tool pointer turns to an arrowhead, the first anchor point appears. Only when you begin to drag it does the cursor change.
3. Drag to adjust the curve segment's slope, then let go of the mouse button. Extending the direction line approximately one-third of the distance to the next anchor point you intend to draw is often a smart practice. Later on, you can modify one or both of the direction line's sides.

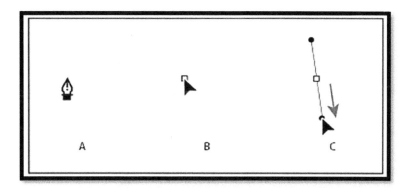

Drawing the first point in a curve

4. Press and hold the Shift key to limit the tool's range to multiples of 45°.

5. Select the endpoint of the curve segment by positioning the Pen tool there. There are two ways that you may make various kinds of curves.

   - Drag in the opposite direction of the previous direction line to make a C-shaped curve, then let go of the mouse button.

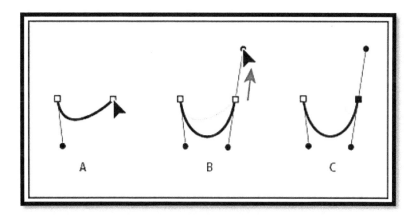

Drawing the second point a curve

   - Drag in the same direction as the preceding direction line, then let go of the mouse button to form an S-shaped curve.

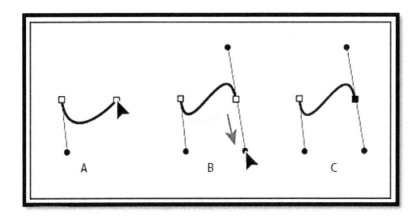

Drawing an S-curve

Note: Release the mouse button, then use the Alt or Option keys to drag the cursor in the curve's direction to make a drastic shift in direction. Release the mouse button and the Alt (Windows) or Option (Mac OS) keys, move the cursor to the desired end of the segment, and drag it in the other way to finish the curve segment.

6. To make a sequence of rounded curves, keep dragging the Pen tool from various places. Make sure that anchor points are positioned at the start and finish of each curve rather than at the curve's tip.

NB: Use the Alt-drag (Windows) or Option-drag (Mac OS) keyboard shortcuts to separate an anchor point's direction lines.

7. **To complete the path, you have two options:**
   • Place the Pen tool over the first (hollow) anchor point to close the route. When you place the Pen tool cursor appropriately, a little circle appears next to it. Drag or click to end the route.
   • You can choose an alternative tool or Ctrl-click (Windows) or Command-click (Mac OS) anywhere away from any items to leave the route open.

Draw straight lines followed by curves.

Photoshop's Pen tool allows you to combine straight lines and curves in one easy step. These are the actions.:

1. Select the initial anchor point where you want the straight section to begin by clicking with the Pen tool.

2. 2. To set the straight segment's endpoint, click once more at a different spot. In doing so, a straight line that connects the two anchor points is produced.

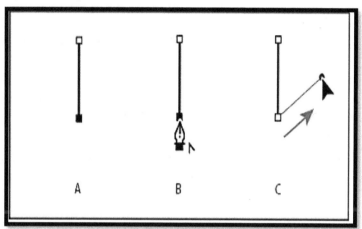

3. Place the Pen tool on the endpoint where the curved segment should begin. You'll see that the Pen tool has a little diagonal line (slash) next to it.

4. Click the anchor point and drag the direction line that appears to adjust the curved segment's slope and direction.

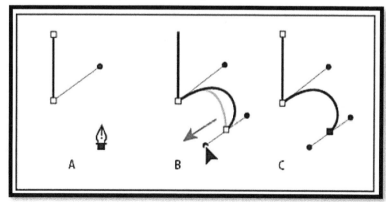

(Visual: Picture demonstrating the initial straight segment's generation, the curved segment's Pen tool placement, and the direction point's dragging)

5. Next, select the location for the curve's next anchor point using the Pen tool.

6. Click on this newly created anchor point. You may move it to change the curve if necessary. The curved section is finished with this operation.

(Visual: Image displaying the finished curved segment and the location of the new anchor point)

Draw curves followed by straight lines

Use the Pen tool to draw a curved segment by doing the following steps:

1. To construct the initial smooth point of the curved section, click and drag the Pen tool while it is chosen. To set the starting curve, release the mouse button.

2. To finish the curve, move the Pen tool to the desired location and click and drag to finish the section. To complete the contour of the curve, release the mouse button.

3. Choose the "Convert Point" tool from the toolbox to change the curve's terminus from a smooth point to a corner point. To initiate the conversion, click on the chosen endpoint.

While using the Pen tool, you may quickly switch to the "Convert Point" tool by hitting Alt (Windows) or Option (Mac OS).

4. Choose the Pen tool from the toolbox once the endpoint has been converted to a corner point. To make the straight section, position it where you want it to terminate and click.

Draw two curved segments connected by a corner.

Use the Pen tool to draw two curved segments joined by a corner point by following these steps:

1. Drag to make the initial smooth point for the first curved section while the Pen tool is chosen.

2. To make the second smooth point for the same curved section, reposition the Pen tool. To set the slope for the following curve, drag the direction line to the opposite end while holding down Alt (Windows) or Option (Mac OS). Let go of the mouse button and the Alt/Option key.

Through the division of the direction lines, the smooth point becomes a corner point.

3. To finish the second curved segment, move the Pen tool to the desired location and drag a new smooth point.

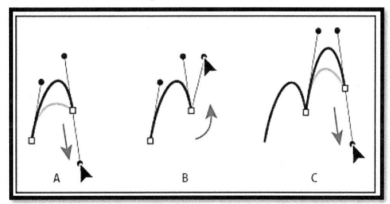

Finish drawing a path.

Use the following Method to finish drawing a path:

1. Place the Pen tool on top of the initial anchor point, which is hollow. There's a little circle next to the Pen tool pointer when it's

positioned appropriately. Thereafter, you may shut the route by clicking or dragging.

2. To maintain an open path, click any place that is not in the path of any objects with the keyboard shortcut Ctrl-click (Windows) or Command-click (Mac OS). As a result, the path will remain open, allowing you to carry out more project components.

How to change image resolution using Adobe Photoshop

Here's a guide on how to change image resolution using Adobe Photoshop:

1. Open Adobe Photoshop and load your image by going to "File" > "Open" and selecting your image.

2. Select "Image Size" from the "Image" menu."

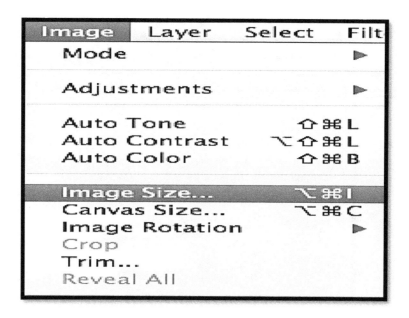

3. The "Image Size" dialog box will show up.

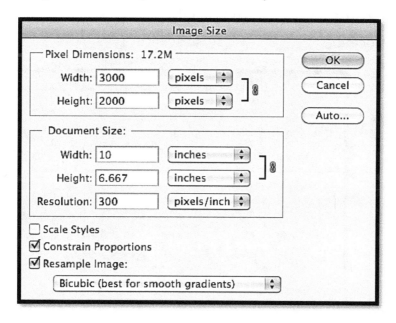

4. Select "Resample Image" and uncheck it to change the resolution solely. This instructs Photoshop not to alter the image's pixel composition. Instead of modifying the image's size, your attention is on adjusting the number of pixels shown per inch (PPI).

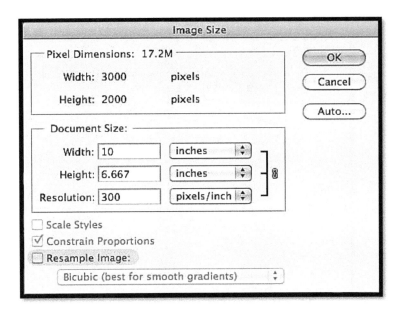

5. Type the resolution value you want in the "Resolution" column. The document's width and height will adjust appropriately as you proceed.

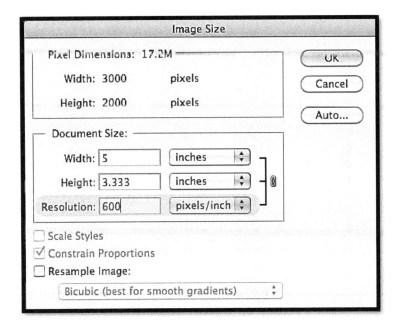

6. Click "OK" to confirm the changes.

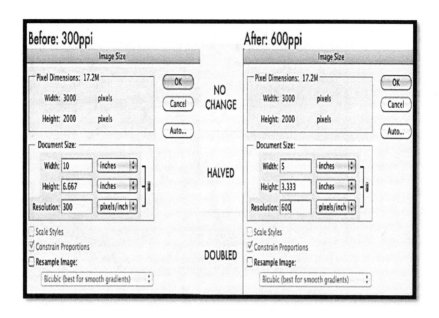

The resolution of the original image in this example was 300 PPI. At 600 PPI, we enhanced the resolution to adhere to the professional publication guidelines. Importantly, the pixel dimensions remained unchanged and no additions nor subtractions were made. However, notice that when the resolution was doubled, the document's height and width were cut in half. Consequently, the image resized to 5" x 3.333" at 600 PPI from 10" x 6.667" at 300 PPI. This shows that the image may be reproduced up to a maximum size of 5" x 3.33" at 600 PPI without losing any quality.

Resolution for Printing

What effect does resolution have on printing? Let's look at an example where we are utilizing a laser printer to produce a picture on typical 8.5 × 11-inch sheets of paper:

1. **72 PPI:** The document will clip because it is too big to fit on an 8.5 x 11-inch sheet at this resolution. Because of the really poor print quality, the image seems exceedingly fuzzy or "soft.".

2. **150 PPI:** The quality is unimpressive and the page size is still too huge for the 8.5 x 11-inch sheet. Although it appears acceptable, the image isn't appealing.

3. **300 PPI**: Almost the whole sheet of paper is occupied by the image, and the print quality is excellent, with sharp, clear details.

4. **600 PPI**: The image is significantly smaller than the previous files, despite the exceptionally high quality.

Which resolution, therefore, ought you to select? Not suited for producing a high-quality print, the 72 PPI and 150 PPI photos are of insufficient quality. Although the 600 PPI image is slightly smaller than the 300 PPI image, both seem sharp. Due to its higher print size and superior quality in this instance, the 300 PPI picture is the recommended option.

When printing images, the key is to find the optimal resolution that achieves the desired size and quality.

Top tips on changing image resolution

1. Examine the dialog box for image size.

You may adjust an image's width, height, or resolution—measured in pixels per inch, or PPI—by choosing Image › Image Size. This will result in a permanent modification to the picture file's size.

2. Decide on a measurement unit.

Click the drop-down menu next to the Width or Height entry to change the unit of measurement. Select from pixels, inches, centimeters, percentages of the original size, and more.

3. Employ the Export feature.

Select File › Export. to create a new, smaller file while maintaining the image's original size. Here's how to use Photoshop to reduce the size of photos without compromising on quality. Additionally, you may use the Export function to export as a lower-quality JPEG, modify the pixel count, or scale down by a percentage.

4. Achieve the ideal quality.

You may modify the zoom level of your scaled picture using the Export As or Picture Size dialog boxes to ensure that it contains the right amount of information for your use case.

CHAPTER FIVE

HOW TO SAMPLE AN IMAGE SIZE

Making changes to the Pixel dimensions of an image

A picture's pixel measurements can affect an image's onscreen size as well as its quality and printed characteristics, such as printed dimensions or resolution.

1. Select Image > Image Size from the Photoshop menu.
2. Choose "Constrain Proportions" to preserve the existing aspect ratio or the correlation between pixel width and pixel height. This guarantees that when you modify the height, the width will adapt automatically.
3. Enter the Width and Height values in the "Pixel Dimensions" box. By selecting "Percent" as the unit of measurement, you can choose to work with percentages of the present dimensions. The Image Size dialog box's top row will show the image's new file size, with the previous file size included in brackets.
4. Make sure "Resample Image" is selected, then choose an interpolation technique.
5. To resize the effects in the edited image, select "Scale Styles" if your image has layers with styles applied to it. This option is only accessible when the option "Constrain Proportions" is chosen.
6. Click "OK" after configuring the necessary parameters."

Change the print dimension and resolution.

Defining the picture size in terms of its printed dimensions and resolution is crucial when producing an image for print media. These two values, together called the document size, establish the total number of pixels in the image, which in turn determines the file size.

The basic size at which an image is incorporated into another program is also determined by the document size. The Print command allows you to further modify the printed picture's scale, but it's important to remember that any modifications you make here only affect the printed image and not the image file's document size.

If you activate the image's resampling, you may change the print size and resolution separately, which will change the number of pixels in the image overall. In contrast, if you disable resampling, Photoshop will automatically update the other value to preserve the total number of pixels even if you modify the dimensions or the resolution.

It's recommended to adjust the dimensions and resolution without resampling at first, and only use resampling when necessary for the greatest print quality.

Here's how to do it:

1. Select Image > Image Size.
2. Change the picture resolution, the print size, or both:
   - Choose a Resample Image and an interpolation method to adjust the print size or resolution while adjusting the overall pixel count proportionately.
   - Uncheck the Resample Image to modify the print size and resolution without influencing the overall number of pixels.
   - Select Constrain Proportions to preserve the image's existing width-to-height aspect ratio. The width is automatically adjusted by this option when you change the height.

3. Enter the updated height and width numbers under Document Size, and if necessary, choose another unit of measurement. The width and gutter sizes indicated in the Units & Rulers preferences are used when selecting the "Columns" option for width.

4. Enter a new number for Resolution and, if required, select an alternative unit of measurement.

How can a picture be resized in Photoshop without influencing its Quality

This method will enable you to change the image's size without affecting its quality or minute features:

1. Save time and storage space through image resizing.

- Photoshop makes it easy to resize images by adjusting the pixel dimensions without sacrificing quality. Larger or higher-resolution photos, or images with more pixels, might need a lot of storage space and a lengthy download time. If the intention is to share the photograph for quick viewing or post it on a digital platform, it is imperative to use a lower-resolution shot with a smaller file size.

2. Examine the dialog box for image size.

- To change the image's width, height, and resolution (measured in pixels per inch, or PPI), select Image > Image Size. Keep in mind that these changes will permanently change the picture file's dimensions.

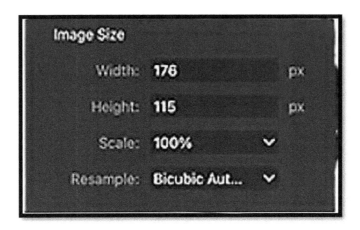

Image Size

Width: 176 px

Height: 115 px

Scale: 100%

Resample: Bicubic Aut...

3. Choose your unit of measurement.

- Click the dropdown menu next to Width or Height and select the desired option to modify the unit of measurement. There are many other units to choose from, including pixels, inches, centimeters, percentages of the original size, and more.

4. Make use of the Export feature.

- Implement the following steps to guarantee that the image quality is preserved and the file size is decreased without sacrificing quality:
- Click "File" and then pick "Export As."
- The save tool allows you to alter the pixel measurements, resize the image by a percentage, and save it as a lower-quality JPEG.

5. Achieve the desired quality.

Change the zoom level in the Export As or Image Size dialog boxes to ensure that the scaled image has the correct amount of detail for your specific need.

Changing the size of a picture with the use of the transform tool

To resize an image using the Transform tool, follow these steps:

1. Click on the picture.
2. Press Ctrl + T (Cmd + T on Mac) to choose the Transform tool. Moreover, Edit > Free Transform gives you access to it.
3. To keep the image's aspect ratio, drag one of the transform box's corners while holding down the Shift key.
4. To resize the picture proportionately, type a percentage in the options bar's Width or Height area. The scrubby slider may be used to change the size, or you can provide a precise pixel value.
5. Hit Return or Enter to apply the change.

Alternatively, use this method to Change the size of a picture with the use of the transform tool.

- Click on the Move tool after selecting the toolbar on the right.
- Select the "Show Transform Controls" option from the Options menu"
- Click on the bounding box surrounding the layer to select it.
- Enter the desired width and height percentages to scale the layer to a specified value.   Right-click inside the % area to change the unit of measurement to pixels, centimeters, or inches.
- Press Enter or choose the checkmark icon from the menu bar after the resizing is finished.

Resizing a picture using preset Templates

The steps to resize an image in Photoshop are as follows:
- Open the picture in Photoshop.
- Go to Image > Image Size to open the Image Size dialog box.

- Use the Fit To drop-down menu to select from a selection of popular print and web sizes, or use the Width and Height sections to input precise values in pixels, inches, or other units.
- Verify that the Resample option is activated, then choose a resampling method from the menu. The scaling method used by Photoshop decides how many pixels it adds or removes. For instance, you may use Bicubic Sharper to minimize the size of an image and Preserve Details 2.0 to increase it.
- Click OK to save your resized image and apply the adjustments.

How to use an Adobe Photoshop Gradient

The versatile Gradient tool in Adobe Photoshop may be used to quickly and easily create seamless color and light changes inside a picture. It offers a variety of gradients that you can apply to improve or overlay other photos, enabling you to produce visually striking backgrounds for projects such as personalized profile pictures, posters, logo designs, and more. Gradients may be used to create a gradual transition from light to dark or to give subtle touches of color and brightness to certain areas of your image to attract the viewer's attention.

The following procedures will help you use Photoshop's Gradient tool effectively:

1. To begin, decide precisely where you want a gradient to be filled in. If no selection is made, the gradient will cover the whole active layer.
2. Click and hold the Paint Bucket tool to expand the tool menu and get the Gradient tool from the toolbar.

3. Click the gradient icon to enter the Gradient Editor and create a new gradient, or select a gradient preset from the various gradient samples in the options bar. You may also change the gradient type, mode, opacity, reverse, dither, and transparency settings using the options bar.

4. Hover the mouse over the selected area to apply the gradient. You may maintain the gradient at a precise angle by holding down the 'Shift' key while dragging, provided that the gradient remains within multiples of 45 degrees. The gradient's length and direction are determined by where your drag starts and ends.

Make a custom gradient layer in Photoshop.

To effectively use the Gradient tool in Photoshop, consider these steps:

1. **Determine the Gradient Location:**
   - To apply the gradient throughout the whole canvas, go to the top menu and choose New › Layer to start a new layer. Place the layer underneath the layers you want to appear in front if you want the gradient to be in the background.

2. **Select the Gradient Tool:**
   - To use the Gradient tool, click its Gradient icon on the toolbar, which is represented by a rectangle with a gray gradient. Alternatively, to get the shortcut, press 'G'. To reach the expanded tool menu, you may also locate this tool by clicking and holding the Paint Bucket tool.

3. **Define the Gradient Shape and Color:**
   - Select among gradient forms including linear, radial, angular, mirrored, or diamond using the options bar. Use the color

picker in the toolbar, select from your swatches, or use presets to choose the colors you want for your gradient.

4. **Access Presets or Customize in the Gradient Editor:**
   - To launch the Gradient Editor dialog box, click the gradient symbol in Photoshop's upper left corner. This is where you select presets, edit them, and adjust your gradient. If you would want some regions to reveal underlying layers, lower the opacity % in the box below and modify the opacity stops at the top of the color ribbon. The colors of the ribbon are visible through the checkerboard design, which symbolizes transparency. To alter how the gradient colors appear, you may also move the color stops along the ribbon's bottom.

5. **Make Further Adjustments in the Options Bar:**
   - Choose the way you want your gradient to blend in with the overall composition of your picture. Select a blending mode, adjust the gradient's opacity percentage, and experiment with other settings using the options bar at the top of the program. Check the 'Reverse' option to change the gradient fill's color order from left to right. To have a more seamless blending experience, activate 'Dither.' Choose "Transparency" if you want to utilize a transparency mask for the gradient fill. Try varying these parameters and the 'Method' choices to see the visual outcomes.

6. **Draw the Gradient Line:**
   - The gradient may be started by clicking and holding the mouse pointer, then dragging it in the desired direction before letting go of the mouse. In contrast to shorter lines, which result in rapid shifts between hues and tones, longer lines provide more subtle transitions.

7. **Save Your Gradient for Future Use:**
   - If you have a gradient that you like, you may store it for use at a later time. Once your gradient has been named in the 'Name' box, drag it into a separate folder or use the 'New' option to add it to the 'Presets' folder. Click anywhere in the preset list with your right mouse button and select "New Gradient Group" to create a brand-new group.'

Apply a gradient Fill.

Adobe Photoshop's Gradient Tool is a flexible tool that lets you mix different colors smoothly. You may make your unique gradients or select from a range of pre-made gradient fills.

Important Information: Bitmap or indexed-color pictures cannot be used with the Gradient Tool.

Here's how to use the Gradient Tool effectively:

1. Choose the appropriate region of your image before applying a gradient fill to it. The gradient fill will be applied to the whole active layer if no selection is made.
2. Next, from the toolbar, choose the Gradient Tool. Holding down the Paint Bucket tool will cause a submenu with more tool options to display if you are unable to locate the Gradient Tool on the toolbar.
3. You have several possibilities for your gradient fill in the options bar at the top of the screen:
   - Selecting a gradient fill from the extensive selection of pre-made gradient samples is as simple as clicking the triangle adjacent to the sample.

- Alternatively, by clicking inside the sample, you may open the Gradient Editor. Depending on the needs of your project, you may use the Gradient Editor to build a custom gradient fill or use one of the pre-made ones. (See the section on "Create a smooth gradient" for further details on how to do so.)

4. Pick one that indicates how the gradient looks at the beginning point (where you first click or push the mouse) and the finishing point (when you release the mouse). There are many gradient styles available in Adobe Photoshop, each of which transmits a different impact.

- **Linear Gradient**: This style creates a shading effect that runs from the beginning to the conclusion in a straight line.
- **Radial gradient:** The shade pattern produced by the radial gradient radiates in a circular motion from the starting point.
- **Angular Gradient:** This shading technique creates a circular effect by sweeping the color counterclockwise around the starting point.
- **Reflected Gradient:** This gradient option creates a symmetrical look by mirroring the identical linear gradient on both sides of the starting point.
- **Diamond Gradient:** This design has tones that go from the center to the outside corners and resemble a diamond shape.

5. Here are the steps to follow in the options bar:
- Select an opacity and blending mode for the paint. (See mixing modes for further information.)
- Select "Reverse" if you want the gradient fill's color order to be reversed.
- Turn on the "Dither" option for a less banding and smoother mix.

- Choose "Transparency" (see Specify the gradient transparency for more details) to add a transparency mask to the gradient fill.
- From the "Perceptual," "Linear," or "Classic" gradient fill methods, select one.

6. Move the pointer to the appropriate gradient beginning point on the image, then drag it to determine the gradient ending point. Holding down the Shift key while dragging will guarantee that the line angle is aligned with 45-degree intervals.

Improved Gradients

Significant improvements have been made to the Gradients capability, which now has on-canvas controls and an editable dynamic preview that doesn't change the actual picture.

One effective method for quickly designing, previewing, and adjusting gradients is the Gradient Tool in the most recent version of the Photoshop desktop application. Color stops may be made and altered right on the canvas with this tool. Additionally, the gradient's color, density, opacity, and blending mode may all be adjusted.

The Gradients feature is set as the default option (no action is needed unless you prefer the Classic gradient).

When working with a pixel layer, you have the choice between two destructive working methods: Classic gradient mode and non-destructive gradient mode. Whether working with a gradient fill layer or a mask, the tool will decide which mode to use automatically based on the kind of layer that is selected.

To make use of the Gradients functionality, take the following actions:

1. Select the canvas area, then drag the gradient on-canvas widget out. You may freely change the gradient's length and angle while dragging. You may click and drag again to return and adjust the length and angle after releasing the drag.

2. Use the mouse to drag and click the diamond-shaped icons to change the midpoints between color stops.

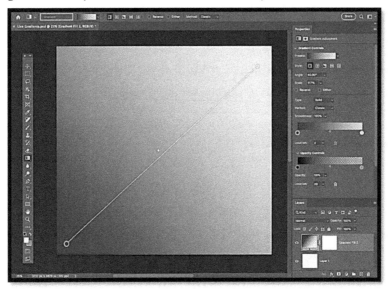

3. Select the color stop circles and drag them away from the gradient line to remove color stops from the on canvas widget. Double-click the color stops (in the circular region) of the Gradient on-canvas widget to use the color picker to change the color.

4. choose a gradient preset from the Properties tab or the dropdown menu.

Add a Gradient to a mask.

To add a gradient to a mask, follow these steps:

1. Select a region of your picture and use the Gradient Tool to apply a gradient to the mask there.

2. To apply the gradient, drag your cursor over the chosen region. The altered mask is then visible in the Layers panel's gradient thumbnail.
3. Choose from a variety of gradient fill types (see "Apply a gradient fill") and move your cursor over the selection a few times to fine-tune it.

Add a Gradient to a smart filter (mask)

To add a gradient to a smart filter, follow these steps:

1. Start by giving your smart object a filter.
2. To apply the gradient, use the Gradient Tool after selecting the Smart Filters thumbnail.
3. To apply the gradient to the smart filter, drag your cursor over the canvas. Observe the thumbnail as it changes.
4. Play around with the different Photoshop filters and drag the widget around the canvas to create different effects. There are more changes you can make, like changing the halfway point.

Apply gradients to layers.

There are several ways to apply a gradient as a layered effect to text layers:

Click on any gradient in the Gradients panel to apply a gradient after selecting one or more text layers from the Layers panel. Another way to apply a gradient is to drag it straight from the Gradients panel onto a layer in the Layers panel or text inside the canvas area.

To apply a gradient as a fill layer to text layers or a shape layer, you can use any of the following methods:

1. Toggle a gradient from the Gradients panel onto the text inside the canvas area by holding Command (Mac) or Alt (Win).
2. Toggle a gradient from the Gradients panel onto a layer in the Layers panel by holding Command (Mac) or Alt (Win).

To apply a gradient to a shape layer as shape fill, follow one of these methods:

1. To apply a gradient as shape fill, choose one or more shape layers in the Layers panel. Next, select a gradient from the Gradients panel.
2. To utilize a gradient as the shape fill, drag and drop it from the Gradients panel onto the canvas area's shape content.
3. Select a layer in the Layers panel and drag a gradient from the Gradients panel onto it. By doing this, the gradient will be applied to the chosen layer's shape fill.

For applying a gradient to pixel layers, follow this process:

Drag and drop a gradient onto a Layers panel pixel layer by dragging it from the Gradients panel.

Photoshop will automatically build a fill layer atop a pixel layer when you apply a gradient to a pixel layer.

Organize gradient presets into groups

To organize your gradients into a new group, follow these steps:

1. Select Window > Gradients to bring up the Gradients panel.
2. In the Gradients panel, select the "Create New Group" icon.
3. Give the group a name, then choose "OK."

4. You may drag and drop gradients into this new group or pick several gradients and add them to the group by using the Shift key.

If you want to create nested groups, here's how to do it:

1. Go to the Gradients tab and choose an existing group.
2. You may create a layered structure for your gradient arrangement by dragging and dropping that group below another group.

How to set up and align thumbnails in Adobe Photoshop on a page

Layer distribution and alignment features are available in Adobe Photoshop. Using a basic picture as our example, we will insert thumbnail images, aligning and distributing them along the right side.

1. Go to File > Place Embedded to import the thumbnail pictures.

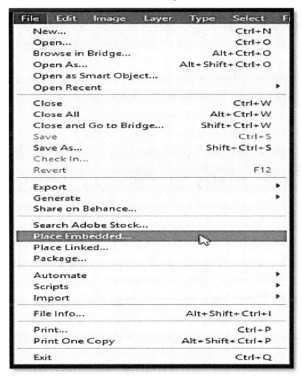

2. Click OK after selecting the pictures you wish to use. You must hit Enter (PC) or Return (Mac) to complete the Place command for each picture you want to enter. They will be added to the Layers panel as separate layers and arranged in a stack inside the picture window. Layers Panel and Picture Positioning.

3. Select the layer in the Layers menu that has the picture thumbnail you want to be the top layer. Then, drag this picture to where you want it to be in the picture window. This will make it the most prominent image.

4. Select the layer containing the picture thumbnail you wish to place at the bottom from the Layers panel now. To make this image the bottom-most image, drag it to the appropriate spot.

5. Select all of the layers that have the thumbnail photos by navigating to the Layers panel. Start by clicking on the top thumbnail layer, then choose the bottom one while holding down the Shift key. By doing this, every thumbnail layer will be highlighted at once.

6. The Align and Distribute buttons will show up in the Options Bar after you have many layers selected. Click Align Right Edges and then Distribute Vertical Centers to continue.

7. The picture thumbnails are now uniformly spaced and have been correctly aligned.

How to make the most of variable fonts in Adobe Photoshop

Variable fonts are a kind of typeface that uses one file to support several font styles, as opposed to static fonts, which require separate files for every style that is offered. Static fonts cannot precisely alter a font's look, but this technology allows users to declare values for different design axes inside a typeface.

How to use variable fonts on the Adobe Fonts website

Every page on the Adobe Fonts website that features changeable fonts within a font family includes a panel that allows users to alter the font to fit their style as well as an interactive text tool. Users can select from a pre-configured instance for rapid adjustments or start from scratch with a custom design.

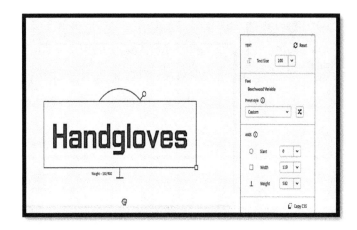

Add variable fonts to a web project.

Click the "Add to Web Project" button, which is situated above the family page's changeable font panel, to store a variable font for your web project. Because some variable fonts include many typefaces in the same family, double-check your font selection.

Then, to copy the code associated with the custom instance you've generated, click "Copy CSS" from the panel's bottom menu. The code must display the default instance in the absence of any custom settings being applied.

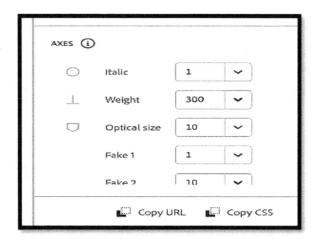

Once a variable font has been customized, you have two options: select "Copy URL" to share or store your configuration, or bookmark the browser's URL to review your most recent custom settings later.

Variable fonts in use

Variable typefaces are incredibly versatile and can be used for a variety of purposes, such as vehicle wrapping, product packaging, and digital graphics. Legibility is ensured even on uneven surfaces when font properties, including width, are optimized.

Variable font settings can be imaginatively configured to communicate a brand's distinct personality or to support long titles, which are sometimes problematic for lower-third images.

Variable fonts offer the freedom to customize the typeface to fit into confined places and unusual forms in packaging design, or to create a visual hierarchy on billboards and posters.

What is monitor Calibration?

The act of adjusting your monitor's color, brightness, contrast, and other settings to conform to a standard or your personal preferences is known as monitor calibration. To achieve precise and consistent color in your visual material, use this technique.

Where to begin your color Calibration?

Color calibration is the crucial step in ensuring that the colors on your printer or screen match their source or your creative vision. Careful color calibration is necessary to preserve consistency and accuracy in color reproduction across a variety of media and devices. In Photoshop 2024, color calibration can begin in several ways to satisfy different needs and preferences. One such method is to use the Colorize filter from the Neural Filters menu. This special feature may automatically colorize black-and-white photographs or alter the color scheme of colorful images with the application of artificial intelligence. Once the filter is enabled, you may adjust the color balance with the sliders on the Neural Filters panel.

White point

The term "white point" describes the hue and brightness of the purest white that a monitor can show.

Gamma settings

Gamma is the brightness of the primary tone in terms of display settings. On a monitor that shows values over the whole spectrum, from black to white, the pattern is nonlinear. They produce a curve on a graph rather than a straight line. The position along this curve, precisely at the halfway point between black and white, is explicitly quantified by gamma.

Luminance

The display's overall intensity level and range, respectively. These settings work just like they would on a television. Using a monitor calibration tool, you may define the appropriate range for brightness and contrast calibration.

Calibrate and profile your monitor

Take into account the following actions to guarantee a successful monitor calibration and profiling process:

1. To ensure a steady output, let your monitor warm up for at least thirty minutes.
2. Verify that the display settings on your monitor are set to thousands or more of colors, preferably millions of colors (24-bit or greater).
3. Clear off any brilliant patterns or bright colors from your monitor's desktop wallpaper and set it to show neutral grays instead. Brilliant patterns and bright colors might skew your sense of color.

For monitor calibration and profiling:

- Use the monitor calibration tool in Windows.
- Use the Calibrate tool in Mac OS. Go to System Preferences, Displays, Color tab.

To achieve the best results, use third-party software and measuring tools. Using a colorimeter or other similar instrument in conjunction with software can produce more accurate profiles because these tools can measure displayed colors more accurately than the human eye.

How often should you calibrate?

Regular monitor calibration should be carried out, preferably once a month. Furthermore, it's a good idea to calibrate your monitor if you detect discernible changes in brightness or color on your screen. Maintaining regular calibration helps guarantee that the colors you see on your screen are true to the original. You may use the Color Calibration tool included in the Display Settings or System Preferences menus on Macs and Windows, respectively, to calibrate your display.

Zooming in Photoshop

The Zoom tool is probably the one you use the most, whether you're editing a photo or making a poster. The Zoom tool is an essential tool for your work, whether you need to zoom out to inspect the full image or enlarge a particular area to make sure every pixel is perfect.

Zoom tool

Click the magnifying glass icon in the toolbar to open the Zoom tool and zoom in on a specific region. To magnify an area, just click on it after using the Zoom tool. As an alternative, you may zoom in or out using the keyboard shortcut by holding down the Z key and moving your cursor to the right or left.

Zoom with a scroll wheel.

Moreover, you may quickly zoom in and out with your mouse's scroll wheel. To get closer to your image, roll the wheel forward; to move farther away, spin the wheel back. To activate this function, enter the Preferences panel by pressing Ctrl+K (Command+K on a Mac), then select the "Zoom with Scroll Wheel" option by checking the box. As an alternative, you may scroll your mouse wheel up or down by holding down the Alt key (or the Option key on a Mac).

Resize windows to fit.

You may easily adjust the size and arrangement of windows to suit your needs. To implement the changes, go to Edit › Preferences › Interface, set the UI Scaling to 100%, and restart Photoshop. As an alternative, you may move and resize windows with the keyboard commands Alt+F7 and Alt+F8.

Zoom all Windows

Select the Zoom tool, then from the Options bar at the top of your project window, select Zoom All Windows to apply the Zoom feature to all open pictures.

Animated and scrubby zoom

These zoom techniques are meant to streamline your process and cut down on the number of unnecessary keystrokes required. Pressing Z to choose the Zoom tool and then clicking and holding on the area of the picture you want to zoom in on will enable Animated Zoom. The longer you hold down the mouse button, the more the image will zoom in. (To activate Animated Zoom, select Tools under Photoshop Preferences). As an alternative to Scrubby Zoom, you may choose the Zoom tool and then zoom in or out by clicking and dragging to the right or left. (When the Zoom tool is chosen, tick the option in the Options bar at the top of your project window to enable Scrubby Zoom.)

Fit screen

Simply choose View › Fit on Screen or press the keyboard shortcuts Command+O (for Mac) or Ctrl+O (for Windows) to quickly resize the picture to fit your screen.).

Using the Zoom tool

These are the methods how to use the Zoom tool:

Display images at 100%

When "100%" is selected, the image will be instantaneously zoomed to 100% of its actual size, with each pixel taking up one pixel on the screen. You can attentively inspect all of the image's minute features at this zoom level. It also indicates how clear the image will be when printed at full size.

Configure Zoom tool Preferences

Select Edit > Preferences > Tools from the menu bar at the top of the screen. The dialog box labeled Tools Preferences will appear. After making the desired modifications, click OK to save the settings and close the dialog box.

Magnify a certain area.

Click the magnifying glass icon in the toolbar to open the Zoom tool. Next, select the region of your picture that you want to enlarge by clicking on it. As an alternative, you may zoom in or out by dragging the mouse to the right or left while holding down the Z key.

Temporarily zoom an image.

To quickly enlarge a picture, utilize the Animated Zoom feature. This feature allows you to zoom in smoothly by clicking and holding the zoom tool on the image. The image may be gradually magnified till you release the mouse button.

Instantly resize the windows when zooming.

Windows may be resized and adjusted to meet your preferences thanks to this flexible functionality. To use it, choose UI Scaling to 100% under Edit › Preferences › Interface, then restart Photoshop to have the changes take effect. Or, Alt+F7 for window movement and Alt+F8 for window resizing.

Fit an image to the screen.

Choosing "Fit Screen" enlarges the picture to a proportionate size so that it fills the window without being too tight. You can see the entire image in this view as none of the image's edges will be chopped. It is Photoshop's default viewing configuration when you open photos.

The Fill Screen

The image will enlarge to fill the window if "Fill Screen" is selected. However, depending on how large it is, it could crop certain areas of your image to fit.

How to use Scrubby Zoom

When "Scrubby Zoom" is enabled, you may zoom in and out of a picture by clicking on a specific region and using your trackpad or mouse's scroll wheel.

Selecting an area to zoom into your image by clicking and dragging, is possible when the "Scrubby Zoom" option is off. The zoom-in point is shown by a rectangle box created by this action.

Three handy zoom buttons appear in the options bar when the Zoom tool is selected: "100%," "Fit Screen," and "Fill Screen."

How to use the Photoshop hand tool

The Hand tool allows you to navigate your image, giving you the feeling of physically moving a photograph on a desk. You can find the Hand tool in the toolbar, or for an even more convenient option, press the space bar on your keyboard. Here's a quick guide on how to use it:

1. Open an image and use the Zoom tool (Z) to enlarge it.
2. From the toolbar, pick the Hand tool. Your cursor will transform into an icon of a hand, as you will observe. To move your image around, click and drag any place on it. The picture will move in the direction that you apply pressure on it.

When you wish to work on another area of the image, you no longer have to zoom out thanks to this useful function. Alternatively, you may quickly pan to the exact region you want to see.

The Hand tool may still be used to travel around sections of your image that are off-screen when you zoom in past 100%.

Three buttons will appear in the top options bar when the Hand tool is active: 100% (actual pixels), Fit Screen, and Fill Screen. With these settings, you may change the image's magnification while actively using the Hand tool.

Panning and zooming with the navigator panel

The Navigator panel can be used to easily adjust the view of your image by zooming and navigating around it. To use the Navigator panel effectively, follow these steps: Adjust Zoom Level: Drag the Navigator panel's slider left and right to see changes in your image view. Enlarge Image: Maximize the slider to the right to enlarge the image up to 3200%. Pan Around: Hover your cursor over the red rectangle in the Navigator panel to turn it into a hand icon. Use the hand tool to drag the rectangle to pan around the image without changing the zoom level.

What Is Super Zoom In Photoshop?

Super Zoom is a newly introduced feature in Photoshop 2024 that leverages neural filters to enhance image size and quality. To utilize this functionality, navigate to Filter > Neural Filters and enable the Super Zoom filter. You can fine-tune the zoom level and quality slider to achieve optimal results.

Super Zoom is among the various neural filters in Adobe Photoshop that leverage Adobe Sensei AI.

How to Utilize Super Zoom in Photoshop

Step 1: Choose Your Picture Launch Photoshop and open the image you want to work on. I'll use an illustration of a living statue in this case.

Step 2: Navigate to the Neural Filters Panel Select "Filter" and then "Neural Filters" from the main Photoshop menu that appears at the top of your screen."

The Neural Filters panel will appear on the right side of your screen when you take this action. There are several listed filters inside the panel. Find the "Super Zoom" filter and turn it on. You might be asked to download this filter if this is your first time using it. If it's required, Photoshop will give you instructions and provide a download button.

Step 3: Zoom In To zoom in and magnify a specific part of the photo, simply click the "+" (plus) magnification button located below the Super Zoom preview. In this example, I've set the magnification to 3x.

When you move your mouse over the preview picture, the hand tool will immediately appear if you need to move the chosen region inside the preview. The hand tool allows you to change the perspective as necessary.

Step 4: Modifying the Super Zoom to improve the quality of your super-zoomed shot, you have a few options:

- Turn on Enhance Image Details to improve sharpness overall.
- To get rid of artifacts brought on by JPEG compression, enable Remove JPG Artifacts. JPEG files are compressed and lose detail when saved; when super-zoomed, these artifacts may become more noticeable. To make sure you're not losing any crucial information, test this feature by turning it on and off.
- While noise tends to be more visible at higher magnifications, the noise reduction slider can help reduce it in the image.
- As you raise magnification, the Sharpen slider can help you stay focused. It won't, however, improve an image that was sharp or out of focus at first.

- Enabling Enhance Face Details tells Photoshop to accentuate facial characteristics if faces are found in the picture.

Step 5: Output Once you've configured the settings to achieve the desired image quality, proceed by selecting "Output" located at the bottom of the panel.

You have the option to place the zoomed image either on a new layer or in a new document. In this case, I opted for "New Layer."

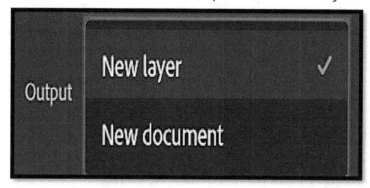

Photoshop will be processing the image methodically, which might take some time. Processing will restart if you want to review and change any of the previously listed settings. Thus, while you're waiting, you might wish to brew a cup of tea. Lastly, press "OK.."

CHAPTER SIX

HOW TO UNDO A COMMAND

Use these procedures to carry out an undo or redo operation

Undo: Reverses a single undo step in the sequence. Use the keyboard shortcuts Ctrl + Z (Windows) or Command + Z (Mac) to select Edit > Undo. Redo: Takes a single stride forward. Use the keyboard keys Shift + Ctrl + Z (Windows) or Shift + Command + Z (Mac) to choose Edit > Redo. Beside the Undo and Redo commands on the Edit menu is the name of the step that will be undone. As an example, Edit > Undo Type of Edit.

Revert to the last saved version.

Reverting to the last saved version in Adobe Photoshop involves the following steps:

1. **Choose File > Revert:**

   - Open the Photoshop interface and select the "File" menu at the top.
   - Select "Revert" from the drop-down menu.

2. **Note on Revert:**
   - Photoshop will restore the document to its previous saved form if you select to revert.
   - To help you monitor the modifications, this action is added to the historical panel as a historical state.
   - Crucially, the "Revert" operation itself is reversible if necessary. This implies that you can go back through your previous states

using the "Undo" feature if you determine the restored state is not what you desire.

Restore part of an image to its previously saved version

The following techniques can be used in Adobe Photoshop to return to a previous state or snapshot:

1. **History Brush Tool:**

   - Click the toolbar icon and choose the History Brush tool.
   - The History panel allows you to select the state or snapshot that you wish to restore.
   - Utilizing the History Brush tool, overlay the image to incorporate the chosen state or snapshot.

2. **Eraser Tool with Erase To History:**
   - Select the toolbar's Eraser tool.
   - The Erase To History option may be found in the tool options bar.
   - The selected state or picture from the History panel may be seen by erasing the image and dragging the Eraser tool over it.

3. **Edit > Fill:**
   - Choose the portion of the picture that needs to be restored.
   - From the menu, select Edit > Fill.
   - Select History under the Use option in the Fill dialog box.
   - To insert the selected state or History panel snapshot into the designated region, click OK.

Note:
   - Ensure that the desired state or snapshot is selected in the History panel before using the History Brush tool or Eraser tool.

- In the History Options, which can be accessible from the Panel menu, make sure the Automatically Create First Snapshot option is chosen to restore the picture to the snapshot of the document's original state. This guarantees that the initial state is automatically preserved as a reference snapshot.

Making use of the history panel

The History panel allows you to return to any previous version of the picture that was produced during this working session. The new state is added to the panel each time a picture is modified.

For example, if you paint, rotate, and choose a portion of a picture, the panel lists each of those states separately. When one of the states is chosen, the image returns to how it looked the first time that particular adjustment was made. After that, you can go on working from that particular condition.

You may also undo picture states from the History panel and, in Photoshop, start a document from a specific state or snapshot.

To access the History panel, either choose Window > History or click on the History panel tab.

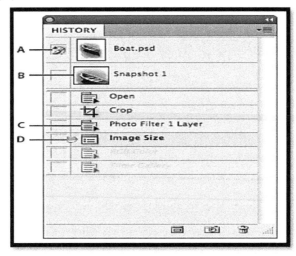

The Photoshop History panel consists of several components:

A. Sets the source for the history brush B. Thumbnail of a snapshot C. History state D. History state slider

Consider the following when using the History panel:

- Since program-wide changes do not pertain specifically to a single picture, they are not documented in the History panel. Examples of these changes include modifications to panels, color settings, actions, and preferences.

- The History section shows the previous 20 states by default. The number of remembered states is modifiable under Performance in the Preferences menu. Photoshop automatically clears off older states to save up memory. If you want to keep a certain state open during your work session, take a snapshot of that state (see "Make a snapshot of an image" section).

- All states and snapshots from the previous working session are removed from the panel when a document is closed and reopened.

- By default, the top of the panel displays the document's initial state snapshot.

- As new states are added, the oldest state is at the top and the newest state is at the bottom of the list.

- The name of the tool or command used to alter the image identifies each stage.

- When selecting a state, the default behavior is to dim the states below it, facilitating the identification of changes that will be discarded if you proceed from the selected state.

- When a state is selected and the image is modified, eliminating subsequent states, the Undo command can be used to undo the last change and restore the deleted states.

- By default, deleting a state removes that state and any subsequent states. If the "Allow Non-Linear History" option is chosen, deleting a state only removes that specific state.

History options

Change the number of entries that may be shown in the History panel, among other configurations, to make it as you want it.

1. Navigate to the History panel menu and choose "History Options."
2. Select an option from the list below:
   - **Automatically Create First Snapshot:** When a document is opened, this feature creates a snapshot of the original picture state.
   - **Automatically Create New Snapshots when Saving:** When you save a document, a snapshot is automatically created.
   - **Allow Non-Linear History:** Allows modifications to a chosen state without erasing subsequent states. This makes it possible to record editing actions in a non-linear fashion, letting you pick a state, alter it, and then remove it without erasing the others.
   - **Show New Snapshot Dialog By Default:** Even when utilizing the panel buttons, this feature prompts for the snapshot name.
   - **Make Layer Visibility Changes Undoable:** Documents changes in layer visibility as they occur in history. By using this option, changes in layer visibility are not included in the history steps.

Edit History Log options.

The Edit History Log in Photoshop might prove to be an invaluable resource if you're required to keep an exhaustive log of all the modifications made to a file. You may use it to establish a textual history of changes, which is appropriate for client documentation, legal needs, or personal records. Adobe Bridge or the File Info dialog box may be used to view the metadata that contains the Edit History Log.

The log information can either be stored in the altered files' metadata or exported to an external file. It's crucial to remember that saving a lot of editing activities as file metadata will make files larger and may affect how long it takes to open and save them.

If you need to prove the integrity of the log file, you may want to consider storing the edit log in the file's metadata and employing Adobe Acrobat for digital signatures for additional protection.

Every session's history log data is automatically stored as metadata that is integrated into the picture file. The location of the history log data storage and the amount of detail that is contained in the history log are both customizable.

1. Open Photoshop > Preferences > General (Mac OS) or Edit > Preferences > General (Windows) and navigate.

2. Select the History Log setting and click on and off as needed.

3. Select one of the following alternatives for the "Save Log Items To" configuration:

   - Stores the history log within each file as embedded metadata.
   - It is possible to export the history log to a text file. Choose a storage location and give the file a name.
   - Both: It creates a text file and stores metadata in the same file.

NB: If you want to save another text file or save the text file somewhere else, click the "Choose" button, give the file a name if needed, and then click "Save.".."

4. Choose one of the choices listed below under the "Edit Log Items" menu:

- Sessions Only: Keeps track of when you launch and exit Photoshop, as well as when you open and close files (including the filename of each image). Omits information on file modifications.
- Concise: Contains data from Sessions and details from the History panel.
- Detailed: Offers a thorough history together with succinct facts and data from the Actions panel. Select Detailed if you want an exhaustive log of all file modifications.

Make a snapshot of an image.

The Snapshot command allows you to temporarily copy any state of the image and add it to the collection of snapshots at the top of the History panel. You can operate from a particular version of the image by selecting a snapshot.

Though they provide extra advantages, snapshots are comparable to the states in the History panel:

1. **Custom Naming:** A snapshot can be given a name for simple identification.
2. **Persistent Storage:** Snapshots are stored for the duration of the work session, providing longer accessibility.
3. **Effortless Comparison**: It is possible to compare impacts with ease. To experiment with different settings, you may switch between snapshots, for example, and take a picture before and after applying a filter.
4. **Work Recovery**: You may easily protect your work by using snapshots. Take a picture before you try out complex methods or perform actions. Choosing the snapshot lets you reverse all actions

and go back to the stored state if you're not happy with the outcome.

NB: Snapshots are erased when the image is closed; they are not kept with the image indefinitely. Furthermore, all states presently presented in the History panel are removed when you choose a snapshot and make modifications to the image, unless you set the Allow Non-Linear History option.

Create a snapshot

Select a state and perform one of the following actions:

1. On the History panel, select the "Create New Snapshot" button to start a snapshot automatically. You may select "New Snapshot" from the History panel menu if the "Automatically Create New Snapshot When Saving" option is activated in the History settings.
2. Select "New Snapshot" from the History panel menu, or Alt-click (Windows) or Option-click (Mac OS) the "Create New Snapshot" button to personalize the snapshot's settings.
3. Type the name of the picture into the Name text field.
4. **Choose the snapshot contents from the From menu:**

   - Full Document Generates a snapshot of the image's layers at that particular point in time.
   - Merged Layers: Creates a snapshot of the image at that point in which all of the layers have been combined.
   - Current Layer: Captures a snapshot of just the layer that is chosen at that particular moment.

Work with snapshots

Choose one of the following actions:

1. To select a snapshot, click its name or switch to a different one by using the slider to the left of the photo.
2. Double-click a photo, then type a new name in the window that appears.
3. Choose the snapshot to be deleted, then utilize the panel menu's "Delete" option, click the Delete icon, or drag the photo to the Delete icon.

How to make a picture straight and how to crop it

Cropping is the process of removing portions of a picture to draw attention to or improve the composition. To trim and align pictures, use Photoshop's trim tool. Because the Crop tool is non-destructive, you may keep the original pixels in case you need to make tweaks later to improve crop boundaries. The Crop tool also has easy-to-use functions that help you correct photographs when cropping.

When cropping or straightening photographs, visual guides provide an interactive preview and real-time feedback to help you see the finished product.

Crop a photo

1. Select the Crop Tool from the toolbar. There will be crop borders around the margins of the picture.
2. Draw or modify the crop limits by dragging the corner and edge handles to create a new cropping region.
3. (Optional) Use the Control bar to define crop choices.

A. Aspect Ratio menu B. Swap Width and Height values C. Overlay Options

Size and proportions: Determine the crop box's dimensions or ratio. Additionally, you have the option to establish your preset settings for later usage, enter your own, or select a preset.

Overlay Options: Select a view to show overlay guidance while cropping. There are available guides such as the Grid, Rule of Thirds, and Golden Ratio. Press O to go through each option one by one.

Crop Options: To define more crop choices, use the Settings (tool) menu.

Use Classic mode: If you wish to utilize the Crop tool, turn this option on.

Auto Center Preview: To position the preview in the center of the canvas, enable the Auto Center Preview option.

Show Cropped Area: Select this option to make the cropped area visible. Only the final area is previewed if this option is deactivated.

Enable Crop Shield: Apply a hue to the cropped regions by using the crop shield. Both color and opacity are customizable. When you alter the crop boundaries, less opacity is shown if you have enabled auto-adjust opacity.

Delete cropped pixels: If you want to perform a non-destructive crop and keep the pixels outside of the crop limits, turn off this option. Pixels are not lost during non-destructive cropping. Later on, you may click on the image to view regions that are not now within the crop borders.

To remove any pixels outside of the crop region, enable this option. It is not possible to make any changes to these deleted pixels later.

NB: Use the context menu by right-clicking the Crop box to view typical crop settings.

4. Press Enter (Windows) or Return (Mac OS) to crop the photo.

Straighten a photo while cropping.

To use the Crop tool to straighten a photo, do the following:

1. Rotate the picture by dragging the cursor just beyond the crop box's corner handles. When you do this, the image rotates following the grid that shows inside the crop box.
2. Alternatively, use the control bar's "Straighten" button. The image may then be straightened by drawing a reference line using the Straighten tool. To match the image with the background, for example, draw a line along the horizon or an edge.

The picture is automatically aligned and rotated throughout this process, and the canvas size is changed to fit the rotated pixels.

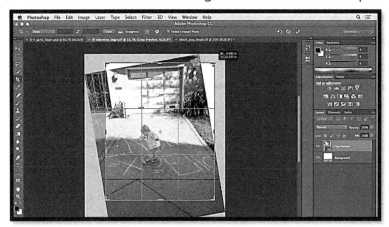

Content-Aware Fill in the crop.

Leverage these methods to exertion Photoshop's Content-Aware technology for cropping and straightening:

1. Choose the Crop Tool from the toolbar.
2. Click the Options bar and select "Content-Aware." The crop rectangle is expanded to encompass the full image when using this default option.

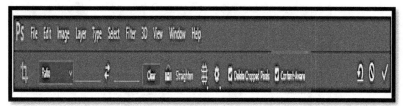

3. Adjust the handles around the image to straighten, rotate, or expand the canvas beyond the original size.
4. Click the Options bar's checkmark button to activate the crop operation if you're happy with the changes. With Content-Aware technology, Photoshop will fill in the blank spaces and gaps intelligently.

Transform Perspective while cropping.

Photoshop's viewpoint Crop tool lets you change an image's viewpoint as you crop it. This is especially helpful for fixing keystone distortion, which happens when taking pictures at an angle instead of directly in front of the subject. For example, the upper margins of a tall structure may look closer together than the lower edges when photographed from ground level.

To use the Perspective Crop tool:

1. Choose the Perspective Crop Tool by clicking on it in the toolbar.

2. To crop and adjust perspective, draw a crop box around the desired cropping region.
3. Rotate the crop box so that its corners match the lines of any structures or objects in the picture.
4. Press Enter on Windows or Return on Mac OS to implement the perspective and cropping adjustments.

A. Original image B. Adjust cropping marquee to match the object's edges C. Final image.

Use these procedures to adjust an image's perspective:

1. Choose the Perspective Crop tool by holding down the Crop tool in the toolbar.
2. Encircle the warped item with a marquee, making sure that its edges match the object's rectangular borders.
3. To complete the perspective crop, hit Return (Mac OS) or Enter (Windows).

How to adjust the canvas size

Use these steps to change the canvas size in Photoshop:

1. Select "Image > Canvas Size" from the drop-down menu.

2. Fill in the Width and Height boxes in the dialog box with the appropriate canvas measurements. From the pop-up choices next to the boxes for width and height, select your desired unit of measurement.

- Choose "Relative" and type in the desired amount to enlarge or reduce the canvas size of the image. To increase or decrease the size of the canvas, enter a positive integer.

2. To specify where to place the current picture on the new canvas using the "Anchor" option, select a square.

3. Select the "Foreground" option to apply the current foreground color to the newly created canvas from the "Canvas Extension Color" menu.

- "Background" to apply the current background color to the newly created canvas.
- "White," "Black," or "Gray" to apply the current background color to the newly created canvas.
- "Other" to use the Color Picker to choose a different canvas color.

NB: The Canvas Extension Color menu is not available if an image doesn't contain a background layer.

4. Click OK to apply the changes.

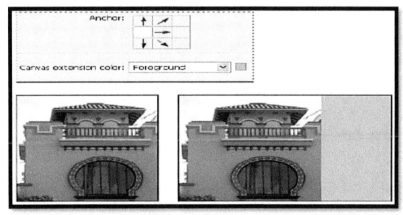

The picture displays the initial canvas on the left and the canvas that was added on the right using the color of the foreground.

Make a frame by increasing the size of the canvas.

Expanding the canvas size and adding color will allow you to construct a picture frame. Or, you may create a themed picture frame by using pre-recorded motions. To protect the original, it is best to work on a copy of your picture.

Follow these steps:

1. Choose Window > Actions to bring up the Actions panel.
2. Select Frames from the menu in the Actions panel.
3. Choose a list item for a frame action.
4. Click the Play Selection button.

A frame will be created around your photo when the selected action is executed.

How to add photos as layer design

When you add an image to a layer in Photoshop, you have more flexibility to manipulate the image and choose how it should fit into the composition overall. A key component of Photoshop picture editing is learning how to add images as layers. One may perform a multitude of creative jobs, including masking, double exposures, collages, and more, by combining layers to blend photographs.

Drag and drop

Dragging an image or photo onto the canvas in Photoshop is the easiest approach to making it a layer. Immediately, the program will create a new layer for the imported picture.

Place and embedded or linked object

Navigate to File › Place Embedded to insert an embedded or linked item. Recall that any modifications you make to the original linked picture will cause it to update instantly in its connected location.

Import from a scanner or other device

Choose File › Import › Images from Device from the menu bar to import images from a scanner or similar device. This lets you import images straight from a camera, scanner, or other devices that are connected.

Copy and paste

If you want to add your image to a new layer, you can copy and paste it by right-clicking and using Command + C on macOS or Ctrl + C on PC. Subsequently, navigate to the desired layer and use Command + V on macOS or Ctrl + V on PC to paste the image.

How to adjust the layer size

It's easy to resize a layer in Photoshop by using the Free Transform tool. Follow these four simple actions to get started:
1. **Select the Layer:** Drag and drop the layer or layers you want to resize from the Layers panel.
2. **Initiate Transformation:** Navigate to Edit › Free Transform.

3. **Resize and Adjust:** To resize or rotate the content as necessary, click and drag the corners or edges of the Transform border while holding down the Shift key to preserve proportions.
4. **Apply Changes**: Apply and complete your changes, press Enter on Windows or Return on macOS.

How to adjust brightness and contrast

The Brightness/Contrast adjustment in Photoshop allows you to make simple tonal adjustments to your image. Follow these steps to fine-tune the brightness and contrast:

1. **Access the Adjustment**: Navigate to the "Image" option after opening your image in Photoshop. After selecting "Adjustments," select."
2. **Adjust Brightness:**
   - Tonal values may be increased and image highlights can be improved by dragging the Brightness slider to the right.
   - Move the Brightness slider to the left to decrease values and emphasize shadows.
3. **Adjust Contrast:**
   - Slide the Contrast slider to the right to increase the tonal range overall, bringing out the details in dark and bright places.
   - Move the Contrast slider to the left to compress the tonal range, reducing the difference between dark and bright areas.
4. **Choose Mode:**
   - Similar to adjustments for levels and curves, modifications in normal mode are proportional and nonlinear.

- "Use Legacy" is an option if you need a more straightforward pixel value shift, however, it's not advised for photographic photos since it might result in clipping or loss of detail.

5. **Apply the Adjustment:** To alter the brightness and contrast of your image, click "OK". For the desired result, adjust as necessary.

6. Use Smart Objects and layer masks to alter your layers

Modify your layers with Smart Objects and layer masks.

The Layers panel functions as the main control center for your workspace, including options for adding new items, modifying the background layer, and enhancing already existing layers. The following are essential features that can improve your editing experience:

Smart Objects: Smart Objects allow for adjustments and transformations without affecting resolution or causing irreversible changes. Photoshop creates Smart Objects from embedded objects automatically. You can:

- Scale, rotate, skew, distort, or warp a layer without erasing the original picture data by using Smart Objects
- Use vector graphics from programs such as Adobe Illustrator.
- You may apply and adjust filters without causing any damage to the original.
- If possible, use resized photos in your layout design that are of lower quality.

NB: You cannot change the pixel data in Smart Objects. The Smart Object has to be rasterized—that is, changed from vector to pixel graphics—to make use of features like blend modes. By choosing "Rasterize Layer," you may make changes at the pixel level to a layer.

Layer Masks

Layer masks offer an adaptable method for going back to certain stages of your editing to correct mistakes or undo modifications. Layer masks hide pixels rather than permanently removing them. To initiate a layer mask, first, choose a layer from the Layers panel:

- In the Layers panel, choose a layer.
- Press the "Add Layer Mask" button, which is situated at the panel's bottom.

A white layer mask is made automatically. The color scheme for dealing with layer masks is white, black, and gray. Using the Brush tool, paint a mask white to expose the layer and black to hide it. You may paint with varied opacity by using gray, which allows for a more sophisticated approach to modifications.

CHAPTER SEVEN

HOW TO ADJUST COLOR VIBRANCY

Vibrancy minimizes clipping by adjusting saturation as colors approach their maximum brightness. After this modification, less intense colors have a higher saturation than already highly saturated colors. Vibrancy also prevents skin tones from being too saturated.

To add an adjustment layer, use one of the following actions:
1. Select Layer > New Adjustment Layer > Vibrancy from the menu bar. Give the Vibrancy adjustment layer a name in the New Layer dialog box, then click OK.

- To add a Vibrancy adjustment layer, click the Vibrancy icon in the Adjustments window.

Additionally, by selecting Image > Adjustments > Vibrancy, you may employ the other technique. Keep in mind that this method removes picture information and modifies the image layer directly.

2. In the Properties panel, use the Vibrancy slider to change the saturation of the colors without worrying about clipping when the colors go close to maximum saturation. Next, select one of the subsequent actions:

- Slide the Vibrancy slider to the right to apply a more significant adjustment to less saturated colors and avoid clipping as they get closer to complete saturation.
- Move the Saturation slider to modify the saturation of all colors uniformly, regardless of their existing saturation levels.
- Move the Vibrancy or Saturation sliders to the left to decrease saturation.

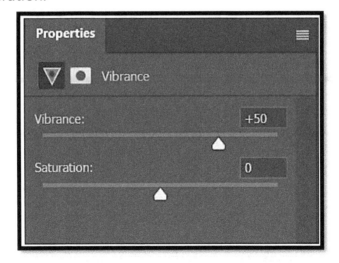

How to modify the saturation and Hue

1. Navigate to the menu bar and choose Vibrancy under Layer > New Adjustment Layer. Give the Vibrancy adjustment layer a name, then click OK in the New Layer dialog box.

Additionally, by selecting Image > Adjustments > Vibrancy, you may employ the other technique. Keep in mind that this method removes picture information and modifies the image layer directly.

2. The following choices in the Properties tab allow you to fine-tune your modifications to Hue and Saturation:

Choose a Preset:

- Choose a pre-established Hue/Saturation setting from the setting menu. For your changes, this provides a convenient starting point.

Adjust Master or Specific Color Ranges:

Select Master, which modifies all colors in the picture at once, is available in the menu next to the on-image modification tool:

- **Choose Master:** This modifies every color in the picture at once
- **Choose a Specific Color Range:** Select one of the preset color ranges for targeted adjustments.

Fine-Tune Color Range:

- Utilize the on-image modification tool to further alter a particular color range. To dynamically change the color's saturation and hue, simply click and drag the picture.

Refine Adjustments:

- Utilize the sliders for Hue, Saturation, and Lightness to make additional adjustments. Experiment with these settings until you achieve the desired color modifications.

Using the Properties panel to access these settings gives you fine-grained control over your image's Hue/Saturation. Selecting certain color ranges guarantees fine-tuned modifications to fulfill your artistic vision.

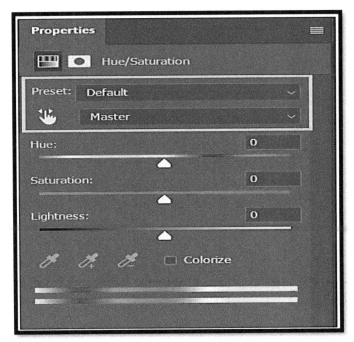

3. Hue Adjustment:

- To adjust the hue, either drag the Hue slider or enter a value until the desired color effect is obtained.

The numbers on display correspond to rotational degrees around a color wheel, with values ranging from -180 to +180. Clockwise rotation is indicated by positive numbers, and counterclockwise rotation is shown by negative values.

- Alternatively, use the On-image adjustment tool:
- Choose the tool and then, on a color in the image, Ctrl-click (Windows) or Command-click (Mac OS).
- Based on the chosen color, drag left or right to interactively change the Hue value.

4. Saturation Adjustment:
- To modify the saturation level, either input a value or move the Saturation slider:
- Drag the screen to the right to enhance saturation.
- Use the left dragging to reduce saturation.
- The values vary from -100 (lower color saturation) to +100 (higher color saturation).
- Use the On-image adjustment tool:
- To adjust the saturation for the chosen color range, click a color in the image and drag it left or right.

5. Lightness Adjustment:
- To change the lightness:
- Adjust the slider for Lightness or enter a value.
- To add white to a hue, slide it to the right to make it lighter.
- Drag to the left to make a color darker (add black to a color)).

Undoing Changes:
- Click the reset button located at the bottom of the Properties screen to reverse the Hue/Saturation settings.

Specify the range of colors adjusted with the use of Hue / Saturation

1. Adjust the Hue and/or saturation.

2. The On-image adjustment button in the Properties tab, and then choose a color from the selection to the right.

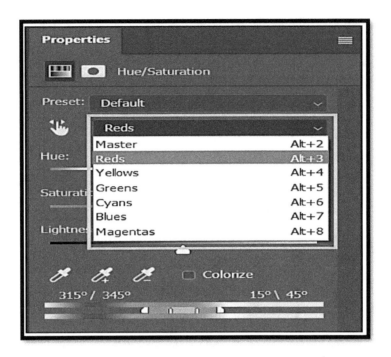

The adjustment sliders are located between the two color bars, along with the associated color wheel values (in degrees).

The color range is set via the two vertical sliders within. The two outer triangle sliders show the point at which a color range's modifications start to taper off or fall out. Fall-off describes the application of changes gradually as opposed to abruptly turning something on or off.

3. Adjust the color spectrum with the adjustment sliders or the eyedropper tools.

- To choose a color range, click or drag within the image using the Eyedropper tool.
- Click or drag the picture using the Add to Sample Eyedropper tool to increase the range.
- Click or drag the Subtract from Sample Eyedropper tool inside the picture to narrow the color range.

- Press Shift to increase the range when an eyedropper tool is chosen, or Alt (Windows) or Option (Mac OS) to decrease it.
- Drag one of the white triangle sliders to adjust the amount of color fall-off (feathering of adjustment) without affecting the range.
- Adjust the range without changing the fall-off amount by dragging the region between the triangle and the vertical bar.
- To choose a new color region, drag the center area to change the adjustment slider in its entirety, including the triangles and vertical bars.
- The color component's range can be adjusted by dragging one of the vertical white bars.
- The color range is increased and the fall-off is decreased by advancing a vertical bar away from the adjustment slider's center and toward a triangle.
- A vertical bar's color range is reduced and its fall-off is increased as it is moved toward the center of the adjustment slider and away from a triangle.
- To change the color of the color bar, you may either Command-drag (Mac OS) or Ctrl-drag (Windows).

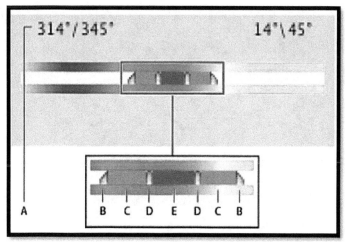

A. Values for the Hue slider B. Adjusts fall-off without impacting range C. Adjusts range without impacting fall-off D. Adjusts both the color range and fall-off E. Shifts the entire slider

When you adjust the slider to transition into a different color range, its name in the menu (located to the right of the On-image adjustment button) updates to indicate the new color range. For instance, if you select Yellow and modify its range to align with the red segment on the color bar, the name transforms to Red 2. You have the flexibility to convert up to six individual color ranges into different variations within the same color range.

How to Unlock the Background Layer

To remove the lock from the Background Layer and convert it into an editable layer:

1. Select Layer > New > Background Layer.

2. Click OK after giving the layer a name.

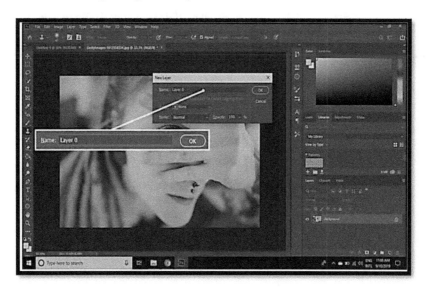

3. The backdrop layer in the palette will be swapped out for the freshly generated and unlocked layer.

Similar to a painting's canvas, the backdrop layer is locked since it forms the composition's basic plane. On top of it are all other aspects. Because of its fundamental function, the backdrop layer cannot have its contents altered or removed, and it is not supported for features like transparency. Furthermore, the background layer's selection can only have one background color applied to it. Edits must be made on a non-locked layer to have total control over how a picture looks.

How to use the quick selection

An image's specified region that you pick for different modifications that allow you to isolate one or more portions of the picture is called a selection. This enables you to alter, add effects, and apply filters to certain portions of your image while preserving the unselected sections.

How to use Lasso tools

The Lasso tool is valuable for sketching freeform segments of a selection border.

1. Select the Lasso tool from the options menu, then play around with the feathering and anti-aliasing settings (see "Soften the edges of selections).

2. Click the matching button on the choices bar to expand, contract, or overlap an existing selection.

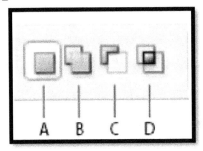

Options for Selection: A. New B. Add To C. Subtract From D. Intersect With

3. Choose one of the following actions:

- Click where segments should start and stop to choose between freehand and straight-edged segments; drag to create a freehand selection boundary. Press Alt (Windows) or Option (Mac OS). Keep the Delete key down to remove freshly drawn straight segments.

4. The selection boundary can be closed by releasing the mouse without holding down Alt or Option.

5. Choose "Select and Mask" as an optional option to further modify the selection border.

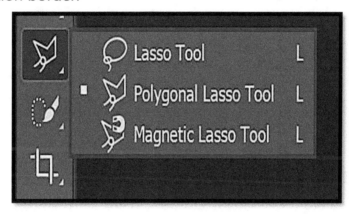

Choose with the polygonal Lasso tool.

Segments of a selection border with straight edges may be easily created with the Polygonal Lasso tool.

1. Select and set the parameters for the Polygonal Lasso tool.

2. Define a selection option found in the choices bar.

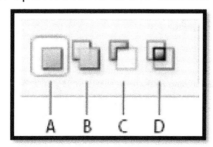

Options for Photoshop Selections: A. New B. Add To C. Subtract From D. Intersect With

3. (If preferred) Modify the options bar's feathering and anti-aliasing settings.

4. To determine the beginning point, click the picture.

5. Select one of the subsequent actions:

- Position the pointer where you want the first straight segment to end and click to draw a straight section. To establish endpoints for the next segments, repeat this procedure.

- Hold Shift down while dragging the mouse pointer to the next section to create a straight line at a multiple of 45°.

- Hold down Alt (Windows) or Option (Mac OS) while dragging to create a freehand section. Release the mouse button and Alt or Option when finished.

- The Delete key can be used to remove recently drawn straight segments.

6. Complete the selection border closure:

- Click after positioning the Polygonal Lasso tool pointer over the beginning point (a closed circle will appear next to the pointer).

- Double-click the Polygonal Lasso tool pointer, Ctrl-click (Windows), or Command-click (Mac OS) if the pointer is not over the beginning point.

7. To make further changes to the selection boundaries, click "Select and Mask" if required.

CHAPTER EIGHT

USING THE MAGIC WAND TOOL

The Magic Wand tool is most effective when applied to images characterized by distinct color contrasts. This optimal condition enhances the tool's accuracy, allowing it to discern and select areas more precisely. When dealing with pictures where colors sharply differ from one another, the Magic Wand tool becomes a powerful partner in your editing.

1. Begin by opening your photo in Photoshop.
2. Locate the Magic Wand icon in the left toolbar (fourth option from the top). If the icon resembles a brush painting a dotted line, right-click and select "Magic Wand Tool."

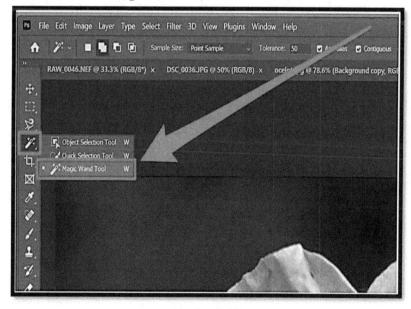

3. Ensure the "Add to selection" mode is selected at the top of the screen. This mode allows you to add to your selection with each click.

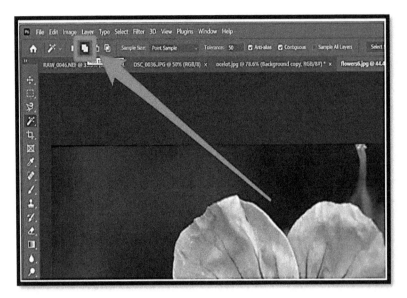

4. Set the Tolerance to "25" at the top of the screen. Adjust this value based on your photo—higher values select more per click.

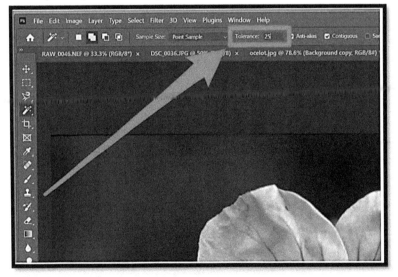

5. Click on the region you want to select in the image.

6. Review the selection. If needed, increase tolerance and try again, or continue clicking to add to your selection.

7. If you selected too much, click the "New selection mode" button (one white square) at the top. Choose a lower tolerance and click again, or use "Add to selection" to refine.

8. Once satisfied with your selection, switch to another tool or use the "Filters" menu for editing. Anything done inside the selection won't affect the rest of the picture.

9. After editing, right-click inside the selection, and choose "Deselect" in the drop-down menu to finalize.

For precision, consider using the Quick Selection tool for additional editing control.

How to use the magnetic Lasso tool

The Magnetic Lasso Tool is a helpful option if you need to make a selection with sharp edges that stand out against the surrounding pixels. To utilize it, take these steps:

1. Launch Photoshop and choose the image you want to edit.

2. Select the Magnetic Lasso Tool from the Tools menu. Usually, it is located on the same menu as Polygonal and conventional Lassos.

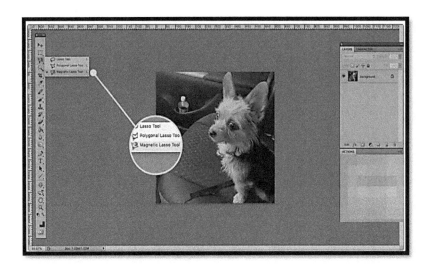

3. The precision cursor, which is a circle with a sign in the center, may be selected by pressing the Caps Lock key in place of the lasso cursor by default.

4. The Tool Options change in the following ways once you activate the Magnetic Lasso too:

1. **Feather**: This parameter determines how far the selection's vignette or blurred edge will extend beyond its boundary. The selection's edge softening is mainly controlled by it. Maintaining the number between 0 and 5 is advised if this is your first time.

2. **Width**: This option determines how big the circle gets when the Caps Lock key is turned on. Using the [or] keys, you may change its size. Notably, this is only an extension of the edge detection area; it is not a brush.

3. **Contrast**: Photoshop recognizes boundaries based on the width of the circle. The amount of color and contrast difference that must exist between an item and its backdrop is determined by contrast. By using the period key (.) to enhance contrast and the

comma key (,) to reduce contrast, you may dynamically adjust the contrast value.

4. **Frequency**: The Lasso tool creates anchor points as you travel across the edges. The distance between these anchor points is determined by the frequency value.

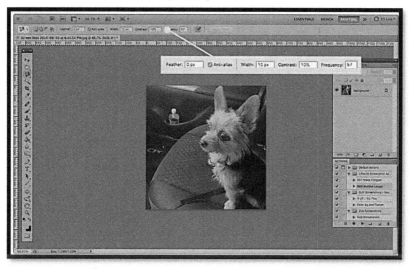

5. Once you've set up your desired settings, click to start the Magnetic Lasso Tool. Move it to the edge of the item you want to pick. Photoshop will locate anchor points (which resemble squares) on its own as you move along the line you trace.

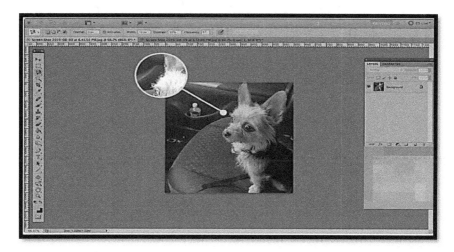

6. Trace the path back to the point where you started the edge tracing and keep going. The cursor will show a little circle in the lower-right corner when it reaches the initial click location, signifying that the loop has finished.

When you click to confirm your choice, a dashed line will appear along the route you outlined in the image.

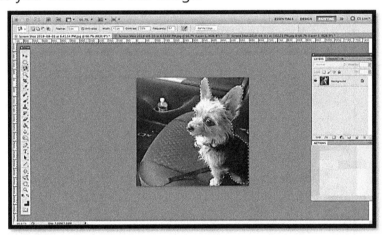

7. You may now manage the choice just like you would with any other. You may move it, fill it in, add a stroke to the selected edge, or duplicate it.

How to use the polygonal Lasso tool

Finding a symbol that looks like a rope with sharp, jagged ends on the toolbar will allow you to use the tool. To define your selection's connection to the other selections, access "Options" and choose from a range of squares. To blend the selected edges, you may also activate feathering and anti-aliasing.

Create Lines around the Object:

- Click anywhere on the object's border to start. To draw a straight line around the entire item with small parts, drag your mouse to the closest corner and click. Continue doing this around the item until the selection is closed. To automatically produce lines at a 45-degree angle, click while holding down the "Shift" key.

Finish the Outline:

- Conclude your selection by returning the cursor to the original starting point. Photoshop displays a closed circle icon, indicating the shape can be closed. Click to finalize the selection.

Use the "Select and Mask" Interface (Optional):

- Choose to access the "Select and Mask" interface by selecting it from the "Options" menu. With the help of this interface's many capabilities for selection refinement—particularly helpful for complex shapes—you may polish your outline.

Types of Eraser Tools

In Photoshop 2024, there are three different kinds of eraser tools: magic eraser tool, background eraser tool, and eraser tool. They are all used for different purposes.

The eraser tool is a simple eraser that replaces pixels with transparency or the color of the background when they are removed. It may be used to remove certain areas from an image or layer or to disclose a lower layer by the erasure of certain areas on a layer to produce visually striking results. The eraser tool's size, hardness, opacity, and flow may all be changed via the settings bar. E on your keyboard or a click on the eraser symbol in the toolbar will choose the eraser tool.

The background eraser tool is perfect for separating subjects from their background by sampling and erasing similar colors. You can use it to remove unwanted parts of an image, such as a sky, a wall, or a shadow. You can adjust the sampling, limits, and tolerance, and protect foreground color options in the options bar. To select the background eraser tool, press Shift + E on your keyboard or click and hold on the eraser icon in the toolbar and choose the background eraser tool from the fly-out menu.

The magic eraser tool erases the selected region instantaneously, yet it functions similarly to the magic wand selection tool. Large sections of solid or related color, like a white backdrop or a blue sky, may be rapidly removed using it. In the options bar, you may change the contiguous, anti-alias, tolerance, and sample all-layer settings. You may either click and hold the eraser symbol in the toolbar and pick the magic eraser tool from the fly-out menu, or you can hit Shift + E on your keyboard to select it.

Eraser with the Eraser Tool

Pixels can be changed to either transparency or the background color using the Eraser tool. Pixels move to the color of the backdrop while working on a background or in a layer with locked transparency; otherwise, they are erased to transparency.

The impacted region can also be returned to a state that you choose in the History panel.

1. Choose the Eraser tool.

2. To erase a backdrop or a layer with locked transparency, set the background color.

3. Select the Mode option from the options bar. While Block is a hard-edged, fixed-sized square without any choices for opacity or flow, Brush and Pencil are similar to those tools.

4. Choose a brush preset and modify Opacity and Flow in the settings bar for Brush and Pencil modes.

   - Pixels are fully erased at 100% opacity, but only partially erased at lesser opacities.

5. Select wipe to History from the options bar after clicking the left column of the selected state or snapshot in the History panel. This will wipe the data to a stored state or snapshot.

NB: To briefly use the Eraser tool in Erase to History mode, hold down Alt (Windows) or Option (Mac OS) while dragging in the image.

6. Drag the region you wish to delete.

Change similar pixels with the magic Eraser tool.

The Magic Eraser tool changes all comparable pixels to transparency when you click inside a layer. When a layer has locked transparency, the color of these pixels becomes the backdrop. When you click on the backdrop, it turns into a layer and all of the same pixels turn translucent.

On the current layer, you can choose to remove all comparable pixels or only contiguous pixels.

1. Select the Magic Eraser instrument.

2. Modify the following options bar settings:

- To find out what color range may be removed, choose a tolerance value. A high tolerance increases the range of colors that will be erased, whereas a low tolerance eliminates pixels with color values that are extremely near to the clicked pixel.
- Select Anti-aliased to soften the erased area's borders.
- Click on Contiguous to delete only the pixels that are next to the clicked one, or pick Deselect to remove all of the image's identical pixels.
- Turn on Sample All Layers to take a combined sample of the color that has been removed from all visible layers.
- To specify the erasing intensity, choose an opacity. A 100% opacity erases entire pixels, but a lesser opacity just partially erases pixels.

3. Select the layer portion you want to remove by clicking on it.

Change pixels to transparent with the Background Erased tool

When you drag pixels on a layer, the Background Eraser tool removes them and makes them translucent. When you want to remove the backdrop from an item in the front while keeping its borders intact, this tool comes in handy. You have control over the transparency range and the borders' sharpness by modifying the sampling and tolerance settings.

NB: If you need to erase the background of an object with intricate or wispy edges, consider using Quick Select.

The color at the hotspot, or center of the brush, is sampled by the background eraser, which then removes that color from the brush wherever it appears. To prevent color halos from appearing when the foreground item is subsequently copied into another picture, it also does color extraction at the margins of any foreground objects.

NB: The background eraser disregards the lock transparency setting of a layer.

1. Select the layer in the Layers panel that has the regions you want to remove.

2. Choose the tool called Background Eraser. (If the tool isn't visible, pick Background Eraser from the pop-up menu by holding down the Eraser tool.)

3 In the pop-up box, adjust the brush parameters by clicking the brush sample located in the options bar:

- Modify the choices for Roundness, Angle, Diameter, Hardness, and Spacing (see Brush tip shape options).
- The Size and Tolerance menus allow you to change the background eraser's size and tolerance during a stroke if you're using a pressure-sensitive digitizing tablet. Select Stylus Wheel to base the variation on the pen thumbwheel position, Pen Pressure to base the variation on pen pressure, or Off if you would rather have no size or tolerance variation.

4. Adjust the following settings in the options bar:

   1. Choose a Limit mode for erasing:

- Discontiguous: Remove the sampled color from any area where it shows up beneath the brush.
- Contiguous: Delete any linked regions that have the sampled color.
- Find Edges: Maintaining the clarity of form edges, erase connected regions that contain the sampled color.

2. **For Tolerance:**
   - Use the slider or input a particular value. While a high tolerance erases a wider variety of colors, a low tolerance restricts erasing to areas that are highly comparable to the sampled color.

3. **Select Protect Foreground Color:**
   - Stop the toolbox's zones that correspond to the foreground color from being erased.

4. **Choose a Sampling option:**
   - Continuous: As you drag, test out colors continually.
   - Once: Only choose the regions that have the color you initially clicked to erase.
   - Background Swatch: Remove just those portions of the backdrop that still have the current color.

5. Drag the designated region to be erased. When marking the tool's hotspot, the Background Eraser tool's pointer will resemble a brush form with a crosshair.

Auto Erase with the Pencil Tool

Painting the background color over regions containing the foreground color is possible with the Pencil tool's Auto Erase function.

Observe these procedures:

1. Identify the colors of the foreground and backdrop.

2. Select the tool for a pencil.

3. Click the settings bar's Auto Erase button.

4. Press and hold the picture.

When you start dragging when the cursor's center is over the foreground color, the region gets wiped to the background color. When you begin dragging over a non-foreground region, the area is painted with the foreground color.

How to use white balance

The process of adjusting color temperature in photography and filmmaking to make white objects look white is known as white balance. It affects your shot's full-color spectrum, though, going beyond just how white appears. Professionals, therefore, carefully arrange each scene, taking into consideration the white balance from the first lighting to the last post-production stages. Get guidance from professionals on how to set, alter, and style this important part of color management so that you can use white balance in your movies more efficiently.

1. Open Photoshop, then select Filter > Camera Raw Filter after opening your image. Choose the "White Balance Tool" from the upper Tools bar of the Camera Raw dialog box.

2. Select Edit > Fill after creating a new layer. Decide to use 50% gray to fill the layer.

3. Choose Difference as the layer blend mode. After adding a threshold adjustment layer, set the threshold level to somewhere between 10 and 15.

4. Press and hold the Shift key while using the Eyedropper tool. To drop a color sample point on an emerging black area, click on it. These areas help provide the best possible color correction since they are closest to a perfect 50% gray.

5. Eliminate the 50% gray layer and threshold. Include an Adjustment Layer for Curves. Click once to use this gray spot to balance the color after selecting the middle/gray eyedropper tool, and zooming in on the eyedropper sample target.

6. The white balance correction that was made using Photoshop and Camera Raw is now visible in your final photograph.

Gauging white balance in various lighting situations

The first step in solving white balance issues on set is to comprehend the color temperatures linked to different types of lighting. It's important to get familiar with common circumstances to properly preserve white balance in situations when you lack control over the color temperature of your light sources unless you operate in a highly controlled setting.

Daylight

In natural light, 5,600 degrees Kelvin (K) is the standard temperature outside. Put practically, you would adjust your white balance to 5,600 K to make sure a white object, such as a sheet of paper, appears properly white in your shot. The color temperature might differ, therefore even though this is the industry standard, it's only a baseline. In contrast to a dark, overcast day, a bright day with a blue sky may feel somewhat warmer. Compared to the noon sun, the color temperature of the sun at sunset and sunrise is often substantially lower.

Tungsten

The normal Kelvin (K) temperature for interior lighting, usually known as tungsten light, is 3,200 degrees. Artificial illumination, such as light bulbs, produces warmer temperatures than outside lighting does. When transferring from an outside to an interior setting, you may reduce the warmer color temperature by adjusting your white balance. Similar to the sun, there are different tungsten settings: warm incandescent lights and LEDs that are closer to room temperature.

Adjust your white balance settings in the camera.

Cameras do not automatically adjust to different color temperatures, unlike human vision. It's critical to set the proper white balance for a scene in your camera. When post-production tweaks may be made to the white balance, it is best to aim for the most accurate white balance possible when filming. By following this procedure, you can ensure that your film has the proper visual data for post-production modifications while also saving time throughout the editing process. Achieving precise accuracy is not the only need for precision. The option to shoot in raw format is a feature that most digital cameras have, giving you plenty of flexibility when it comes to post-processing. It's best to manually adjust the white balance after starting with a preset, such as daylight or tungsten. Here are a few ways to accomplish this, however, there are more.

Learning about color Temperatures

Color temperature is a measurement that takes into account how blue light affects a color's perceived warmth or coolness. A colder tone is produced by more blue light, whereas a warmer tone is produced by less blue light. An image's mood and ambiance are greatly influenced by its color temperature.

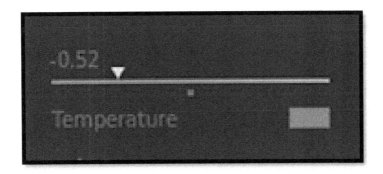

Adjust the Look panel's Color Temperature slider to modify the hue.
Color Temperature Slider:

- Move the slider to the left to decrease the image's warmth.
- Drag the Color Temperature slider to the right to increase the image's warmth.

Color production in Post –Production Editing

Color production is an important aspect of post-production editing in Photoshop 2024. It involves adjusting the color, contrast, saturation, and tone of an image to enhance its visual appeal and mood. Color production can also be used to create different effects, such as stylizing an image, changing the time of day, or adding drama and emotion. Using adjustment layers and layer masks to apply non-destructive edits to specific parts of an image. Adjustment layers allow you to adjust the color and exposure of an image without affecting the original pixels. Layer masks let you control the visibility of the adjustment layers by painting with black and white. You can use different types of adjustment layers, such as curves, levels, hue/saturation, color balance, and selective color, to fine-tune the color production of your image. You can also use blending modes and opacity to change how the adjustment layers interact with the underlying layers.

Color correction

Color correction is the process of altering a picture to balance out and correct color differences seen by the human eye. Digital editing aims to bring the image as near to how we observed it in real life as possible. This is accomplished by making little but effective changes to the image's appearance, feel, and look.

Color Grading

Color grading lets you use your color scheme to create a unified look or mood. Color grading adds a visual tone, as opposed to color correction, which seeks to mimic real-life appearances. Examine the components that you can change or control to give your photos a cohesive, expressive, and creative color grade.

Color Adjustments

Color adjustments are a way of changing the appearance and mood of an image by modifying its colors, contrast, saturation, and tone. Color adjustments can be used for various purposes, such as enhancing the quality of an image, correcting color errors, creating artistic effects, or matching the color of different images.

Correcting Images

Here is the standard process for correcting the tonality and color of an image:

1. Examine the image's quality and tone range using the histogram.

2. To access color and tone settings, make sure the settings panel is open. Select an icon to view the changes described in the stages that follow. An adjustment layer is created when adjustments are applied from the Adjustments panel, offering more flexibility and protecting picture information. See the Overview of the Adjustments panel for more on adjustment and fill layers.

3. Adjust the color balance to correct oversaturated or undersaturated colors and remove undesirable color casts.

4. Use the Levels or Curves settings to modify the tonal range.

To build an overall tone range, adjust the values of the image's extreme highlight and shadow pixels to begin tonal adjustments. Establishing highlights and shadows or figuring out the white and black spots are steps in this procedure. Midtone pixels are usually redistributed correctly by altering highlights and shadows, although manual midtone changes could be required.

Use the Shadow/Highlight command to apply specific tone modifications to regions that are highlighted and shadowed. See How to Improve Shadow and Highlight Detail for further details.

5. (Optional) Make more color modifications.

After your image's general color balance has been corrected, think about applying optional modifications to enhance certain colors or provide unique effects.

6. Adjust the image edges' sharpness.

The next step is to use the Unsharp Mask or the Smart Sharpen filter to make the image's edges more readable. The picture quality produced by the digital camera or scanner being used determines how much sharpening is required.

7. Adjust the picture to the press's or printer's specifications.

To add highlight and shadow details to the color gamut of an output device, such as a desktop printer, use the settings found under the Levels or Curves adjustments. If you know the specifications of the printing press, you may also use this modification while transmitting a picture to it.

Some pixels in important locations may become unprintable on the printer or press in use as a result of the sharpened pixels' higher contrast with nearby pixels. As such, fine-tuning the output parameters following sharpening is recommended.

Adjustment panel overview

The Adjustment panel is the space where you can apply diverse color and tonal adjustments to your image without making permanent changes to the pixel values.

The Adjustments panel contains the color and tone adjusting tools. When you click on a tool icon, an adjustment layer is immediately created in addition to selecting the matching adjustment. Non-destructive adjustment layers are produced as a result of the modifications made with the help of the controls and choices in the modifications panel.

Adjustment presets for Levels, Curves, Exposure, Hue/Saturation, Black and white, Channel Mixer, and Selective Color are available through the Presets option in the Properties panel. A preset may be applied to a picture via an adjustment layer by clicking on it. Furthermore, you may choose to store the adjustment settings as a preset, which is added to the list of presets.

Apply a correction using the adjustment panel

1. Click on an adjustment icon or choose one from the panel menu.
2. Apply the required settings by making use of the Properties panel's buttons and choices.

Perform any of the following actions:

- Toggle Layer Visibility: Click the button to toggle the adjustment's visibility.
- To restore the adjustment to its initial configuration, click the Reset button.
- The Delete This Adjustment Layer button can be used to discard an adjustment.
- Drag the panel's bottom corner to increase the Adjustment panel's width.

Apply a correction to adjust the layer below.

To selectively apply a correction to the layer immediately below in Photoshop, you can utilize a clipping mask. A clipping mask allows you to conceal a portion of an image behind another layer, ensuring that the adjustment layer exclusively influences the layer to which it is clipped.

To establish a clipping mask, adhere to these steps:

1. Verify that the Layers panel has an adjustment layer positioned above the layer you want to change. If not, create one by choosing an adjustment type and clicking the New Adjustment Layer button located at the bottom of the Layers panel.

2. Select Create Clipping Mask from the menu by right-clicking on the adjustment layer. The adjustment layer icon will now show a little downward-pointing arrow, suggesting that it is clipped to the layer below.

3. Use the Properties panel to modify the adjustment layer's parameters until the intended result is obtained. To further hide or show portions of the adjustment layer, you may use the mask thumbnail to paint in black or white.

Save and apply adjustment presets

The Properties panel features a Preset menu containing adjustment presets for the selected tool in the Adjustments panel. Furthermore, you can create and utilize presets for Levels, Curves, Exposure, Hue/Saturation, Black and white, Channel Mixer, and Selective Color. Once a preset is saved, it gets appended to the preset list.

Choose the Save Preset option from the Properties panel menu to save adjustment settings as a preset. Select a preset from the Preset menu in the Properties panel to apply an adjustment preset.

Make a color Adjustment.

The basic operation of all Photoshop color adjustment tools is to essentially remap an existing range of pixel values to a new range. These tools differ from one another in terms of the degree of control they provide. The Adjustments panel provides access to color adjustment tools and the option settings associated with them. See Color adjustment commands for a summary of these tools.

There are several ways to change the color of an image, but using an adjustment layer is one of the more versatile options. Photoshop creates an adjustment layer automatically when you pick a color adjustment tool in the Adjustments tab. You can play around with color and tone changes using adjustment layers without having to make permanent changes to the image's pixel composition. The adjustment layer contains color and tone modifications and acts as a transparent overlay that preserves the visibility of the underlying picture layers.

1. If you want to alter a certain region of your picture, be sure to pick that precise area. Without selecting anything, the entire image will have the modification applied to it.

2. Execute one of the following actions:

- Elect an adjustment by clicking on one of the panel's icons.
- Establish a layer for adjustments.
- In the Layers panel, double-click the thumbnail of an adjustment layer that is already there.

NB: As an alternative, you may go to Image > modifications and make modifications directly to the image layer by choosing a command from the submenu. Note that there is a loss of picture information when using this approach.

When a new adjustment layer is created, its default layer mask—which is initially empty or white—is applied. This implies that your initial modification is applied to the entire image. If there is an active selection while making an adjustment layer, the initial layer mask will mask off the unselected region in black. To precisely manage where the modification impacts the image, paint black areas on the mask using the Brush tool.

3. Click the Toggle Layer Visibility icon in the Properties section to inspect your image with and without modifications.

NB: Click the Reset button to reverse any modifications.

.

Save adjustment settings

These are the methods to apply your saved color adjustment settings to other images:

1. After modifying the color parameters to your preference, select "Save Preset" from the Properties panel's panel menu.
2. In the pop-up dialog box, give the preset a name, and then select "Save.."
3. The Preset option in the Properties panel will now allow you to retrieve the saved preset. By choosing your preferred preset, you may use it on other pictures.

NB: Note: This option allows you to alter Hue/Saturation, Black and white, Channel Mixer, Exposure, Levels, Curves, and Selective Color. Click "Save" in the corresponding dialog box and repeat the procedure for the Shadows/Highlights or Replace Color modifications.

Reapply adjustment settings

These procedures make it simple to reapply an adjustment setting once you've saved it as a preset:

1. From the Preset menu in the Properties panel, select the required adjustment preset.

2. Select "Load" from the adjustment dialog box and find the adjusted file that was saved. Presets menu items will show up in dialog boxes like Curves, Black & White, Exposure, Hue/Saturation, Selective Color, Levels, or Channel Mixer. If you wish to load a preset that is not displayed on the Preset pop-up menu from a different place, select "Load Preset" from the Preset option.

To remove default presets, go to the specified folders, move the presets out of the folders, and restart Photoshop:

• Windows:[startupdrive]/ProgramFiles/Adobe/Adobe Photoshop [version number]/Presets/[adjustment type]/[preset name]

• Mac OS: [startup drive]/Applications/Adobe Photoshop [version number]/Presets/[adjustment type]/[preset name]

Correcting colors in CMYK and RGB

While most modifications may be made in CMYK mode and all color and tone corrections in RGB mode, it's important to select a mode carefully to prevent frequent conversions between modes, which can result in the loss of color values with each conversion. Here are some rules to follow:

1. **RGB Mode:**

   • If a picture is meant to be displayed on a screen, do not convert it to CMYK mode.

- Avoid using RGB mode for color adjustments on CMYK pictures that are going to be split and printed.
- Use RGB mode for most tone and color adjustments; save CMYK mode for the last adjustments.
- Working in RGB mode has several benefits, such as a greater spectrum of colors, improved color preservation after modifications, and fewer channels, which lead to less memory consumption.
- Soft proofing lets you see in real time how the colors in your document will appear on various output devices.

2. **Editing Across Modes:**

- If you have to convert a picture between modes, choose RGB mode for most tone and color adjustments.
- You can examine an image in CMYK colors in one window and modify it in RGB mode in another. Select "Working CMYK" under Proof Setup, open a second window using "Window > Arrange > New Window For (Filename)," and use the Proof Color command to activate the CMYK preview in one of the windows.

These factors guarantee effective color management and avoid needless color information loss during mode transitions.

Using Brushes

Photoshop brushes offer a flexible way to boost your creativity and add variety to your photographs. You may add different creative elements, textures, patterns, and strokes to them. You may get brushes from several locations, such as websites and online markets, or you can make your own to customize your collection of digital tools.

Brush Settings panel overview

Photoshop's Brush Settings panel offers tools for modifying and creating brushes. You may create new brushes and edit existing ones within this panel. It has a range of brush tip choices that control how paint is applied to a picture. The bottom of the panel has a brush stroke preview that shows you how paint strokes will look with the current brush settings.

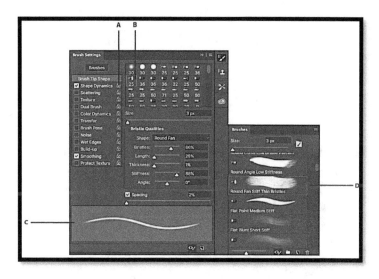

The Brushes panel is located on the right, while the Brush Settings panel is located on the left in the Photoshop Brush Panel.

A. Secured/Unsecured B. A particular brush tip C. Preview of brush strokes D. Panel of brushes

Use these procedures to open Photoshop's Brush panel and brush options:

1. Select Window > Brush Properties. As an alternative, pick a tool for painting, erasing, toning, or focusing, then click the panel button located on the options bar's left side.

2. Choose an option set from the Brush Settings panel's left side. The panel's right side will show the possible alternatives for the selected set.

NB: By selecting the checkbox to the left of the option set, you may activate or disable any item inside the set.

Import Brushes and Brush Packs

The procedures below can be used to import brushes into Photoshop, including paid and free brush packs like Kyle's Photoshop brush packs:

1. Open the flyout menu from the Brushes panel.
2. From the flyout menu, select "Get More Brushes". As an alternative, you may use the contextual menu by right-clicking on a brush shown in the Brushes panel and choosing "Get More Brushes.

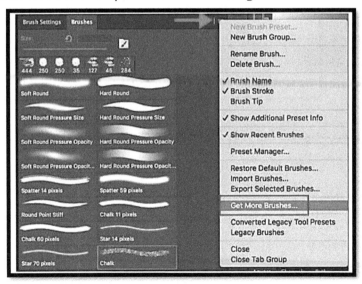

3. Get a brush set, like Kyle's "Megapack.."
4. Double-click the ABR file that you downloaded while Photoshop is open.
5. The Brushes panel will now display the recently added brushes.

NB: As an alternative, you may find and open the downloaded ABR file by using the "Import Brushes" option in the Brushes panel flyout menu. The brushes will be added to your Brushes panel by this operation.

Create a Brush and set painting options

1. Select an eraser, painting, toning, or focus tool.
2. Select Brush Settings under Window.
3. Select a brush tip shape from the Brush Settings panel, or click Brush Presets to choose an already-existing preset.
4. Choose "Brush Tip Shape" from the Brush Settings panel's left-side menu and play around with the settings.
5. Investigate other brush choices, such as adding dynamic components, figuring out how a stroke is scattered, making textured brushes, and modifying how the brush evolves dynamically.
6. For more exact control, think about painting or drawing on your graphics tablet.
7. Click the lock symbol to secure the brush tip shape properties so they are retained when you choose a different brush preset. Click the unlock symbol to reveal the tip.
8. Choose "New Brush Preset" from the Brush panel menu to store the brush for later usage.

NB: Save the brush as part of a collection of brushes for long-term storage or sharing with others. From the Brush Presets tab, select "Save Brushes" and save it to a new set or overwrite an existing set. You risk losing your new brush if you change or reset the brushes in the Brush Presets tab without storing them as a set.

Square Brush

Photoshop's square brush is a flexible tool that may be used for a variety of picture-altering applications. Its square form makes it useful for producing various visual effects in photos by enabling the exact removal or addition of items in a square format.

There's a set of 24 square brushes, all of which are numbered and shaped differently to provide a range of viewpoints. Every brush, which has a number from one (the smallest) to 24 (the biggest), has a distinct function according to its size.

Creating square brushes in Photoshop is an easy process:

1. Launch a fresh instance of Photoshop and choose the 'Rectangular Marquee Tool.'

2. To make a blank square portion, drag your mouse while holding down the shift key.

3. Change the brush's color to black, as this is essential to its operation. You may accomplish this by simultaneously hitting the DELETE and SHIFT keys.

4. Locate the 'Edit' option and find "Define New Brush Preset." Click this option to establish the square brush.

CHAPTER NINE

HOW TO WORK WITH BRUSHES

Choose a preset brush

A preset brush is a brush tip that has been stored and has been assigned certain attributes, such as hardness, size, and form. Tool presets for the Brush tool may now be saved and retrieved from the Tool Preset menu in the options bar. Preset brushes can be saved with commonly used properties. Furthermore, you may use the "Options" bar > "Presets" > "Convert All to Brush Presets" option to convert all Brush tool presets to brush presets. It's crucial to remember that modifications to a preset brush's size, shape, or hardness are just temporary; the original configurations are reverted the next time you select that preset.

The following steps must be taken in Photoshop to choose a preset brush:

1. Open the Brush pop-up menu in the options bar after selecting a painting or editing tool.
2. From the menu, pick a brush.

NB: Another option is to select a brush from the Brush Settings window. Click "Brushes" in the upper-left corner of the window to display the loaded presets.

3. Change the default brush's parameters:
   - **Diameter:** Modifies the brush size momentarily. You can input a value or drag the slider. Both the primary and dual brush tips are scaled if the brush has two points.

- **Use Sample Size:** If the form is based on a sample, then use the brush tip's original diameter. (Not applicable to circular brushes.)
- **Hardness:** (Only available for square and round brushes.) Modifies the brush tool's anti-aliasing amount momentarily. The brush tool is still anti-aliased even when it is painted with the toughest brush tip at 100%. Without anti-aliasing, the pencil always leaves a sharp edge behind.

NB: The Brushes panel (Window > Brushes) allows you to change the preset brush parameters as well).

Manage Brushes and Brush Presets

Grouping your brushes in the Brushes panel can help you arrange them more effectively.

1. Click the icon located in the Brushes panel.

2. Give the group a name, then choose OK.

3. Move presets and brushes into the newly formed group.

Please feel free to create other groups as needed.

Rename a preset brush

To manipulate brushes without any trouble, follow these steps:
Choose a brush in the Brush Presets panel, then click the panel's menu and choose Rename Brush. After putting in a new name, click OK. Double-click a brush tip in the Brush panel, and choose OK after typing a new name.

Delete a preset brush

Easily remove preset brushes in Photoshop using these techniques::

1. Select the required brush by Alt-clicking (Windows) or Option-clicking (Mac OS) in the Brush panel or Brush Preset Picker.
2. After choosing a brush, click the Delete symbol in the Brush panel or choose Delete Brush from the panel menu.
3. Locate the preset manager by going to Edit > Presets > Preset Manager, selecting "Tools" from the drop-down menu, and removing the appropriate brush tool presets.

Create a new preset brush.

In Photoshop, you have to do the following steps to make a new preset brush:

Save your personalized brush so that the Preset Manager and Brushes panel may easily access it

1. Customize the brush to your preferences.
2. In the panel for brushes:
   - Choose "New Brush Preset" from the panel menu, name your preset brush, and then click OK.
   - As an alternative, click the icon for "Create New Brush".

Draw and paint with a mixer Brush.

Photoshop's Mixer Brush replicates real painting techniques by simulating color mixing on a canvas, blending colors with a brush, and varying the wetness of paint during a stroke.

This gadget combines a pickup and a reservoir paint well. With more paint capacity, the reservoir retains the final color applied to the canvas. Only paint from the canvas is received by the pickup well, guaranteeing a consistent mix with the colors of the canvas.

1. Click on the Mixer Brush tool to choose it. (If necessary, to access the Mixer Brush, click and hold the regular Brush tool.)

2. Press Alt-click (Windows) or Option-click (Mac OS) on the canvas to add paint to the reservoir. As an alternative, you may choose a color for the foreground.

NB: Any color differences in the sampled region will be mirrored by the brush tip when loading paint from the canvas. Select Load Solid Colors Only from the Current Brush Load pop-up menu in the settings bar if you want brush tips that are all the same color.

3. Choose a brush by selecting it from the Brush Presets menu.

4. Set up tool choices in the options bar. See "Paint tool options" for a broad list of choices. Go over the following parameters that are special to Mixer Brushes:

- Current Brush Load swatch: Select "Clean Brush" to remove paint from the brush or click "Load Brush" to fill the brush with the reservoir color from the pop-up menu. Select the appropriate option to enable automated loading or cleaning after every stroke.
- Preset pop-up menu: Applies common configuration combinations for Wet, Load, and Mix.
- Wet: Controls the quantity of paint that the brush removes from the canvas. Paint streaks get longer at higher levels.

The amount of paint that is placed into the reservoir is determined by the load. Paint strokes dry faster at lower load rates.

The proportion of reservoir paint to canvas paint in Photoshop is adjusted using the Mix option. At 100%, every drop of paint is taken from the canvas; at 0%, all paint is drawn from the reservoir. You may choose the canvas color from every layer that is visible by using the Sample All Layers option.

5. Complete one or more of the following assignments:

- Drag to add paint to the picture
- Click the beginning point of the picture, hold down Shift, then click the finish point to create a straight line.
- To collect color while using a Brush tool like an airbrush, press and hold the mouse button without dragging.

Stroke Smoothing

Photoshop intelligently smoothes the strokes of your brushes. Choose a Smoothing value (0–100) in the Options bar while working with Brush, Pencil, Mixer Brush, or Eraser tools. The legacy smoothing from earlier Photoshop versions is replicated with a value of 0. Your strokes will be smoothed more intelligently as the settings increase.

Multiple modes of stroke smoothing operation exist. To switch on one or more of the following modes, click the gear symbol:

Paint is only applied in Pulled String Mode when the string is tight. Marks are not left by movements made inside the smoothing radius of the cursor.

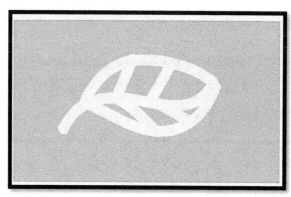

When you pause a stroke, Stroke Catch Up allows the paint to follow your cursor. If it is deactivated, the paint job ends as soon as the pointer moves to the end.

Catch-Up On Stroke End finishes the stroke from the last paint position to the point where you release the mouse/stylus control.

Smoothing may be adjusted for Zoom to avoid jerky strokes. Zooming in on the paper results in less smoothing, and zooming out results in more smoothing.

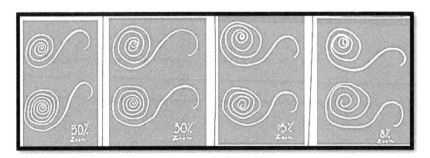

Painting

A multitude of tools are available in Adobe Photoshop for painting and adjusting the color of photographs. The Brush and Pencil tools work similarly to traditional drawing tools in that color is applied using brush strokes. Moreover, tools like the Eraser, Blur, and Smudge tools may be used to change the image's present hues. In each painting tool's options bar, users may change how color is applied and select from a range of predefined brush tips.

Brush and Tool presets

Photoshop brushes and tool presets offer an easy method to store and apply various settings, guaranteeing your photos have consistent and personalized effects.

Specific brush tip properties, like size, shape, and hardness, are stored in brush presets. They can be made from scratch, a picture, or stored with often-used properties. You may also import brushes from other sources, such as online stores.

The Brush tool's settings are saved in tool presets, which are accessed through the Tool Preset menu in the options bar. These presets may be stored for several brush types, such as airbrush, pencil, and chalk. The Options bar's Convert All to Brush Presets option allows you to convert every tool preset to a brush preset.

To use a brush or tool preset in Photoshop, follow these steps:

1. Open Photoshop and make sure your image is in the Layers panel.
2. Select a painting or editing tool from the Tools panel.
3. Select a brush or tool preset by clicking on the Brush pop-up menu located in the options bar.

4. Modify the options in the Tool Preset menu or the Brush Settings panel (Window > Brush Settings).

5. Use the right-click menu to choose Create Clipping Mask when you want to apply the effect to a certain layer underneath it.

6. Use presets for quick, typical modifications by selecting a preset from the menu by clicking on Presets in the Brush Settings panel or the Tool Preset menu.

Brush tip options

Photoshop's brush tip selection is an important tool for adjusting color application, in addition to the settings found in the options bar. Applying color gradually is made possible by these options, which also let you employ a range of curved brushes, soft edges, varied brush dynamics, and different blending qualities. You can even make your brushstrokes look like they were painted on canvas or paper by adding texture or simulating airbrushing with several brush tip settings. The Brush Settings panel is the primary site for configuring these brush tip options. You can apply color with much greater control when you use a drawing tablet. Pen pressure, angle, rotation, and stylus wheel settings are also accessible in the Brush Settings panel and the settings menu, with matching choices found in the Brush Settings panel and the options bar.

Paint with the brush tool or pencil tool.

The foreground color of an image is applied using the Brush and Pencil tools. While the Pencil tool draws lines with a sharp edge, the Brush tool applies color in gentle Moves.

NB: Painting becomes more convenient when the canvas is rotated using the Rotation tool. For further details, see Use the Rotate View tool.

To paint, follow these steps:

1. Select a color for the foreground (Select colors in the toolbox).
2. Choose between the Brush and Pencil tools.
3. Select a brush from the Brushes panel.
4. Use the options bar to adjust tool parameters like opacity and mode.
5. **Perform one or more of the following actions:**
    *   To add paint to the picture, click and drag.
    *   Click an image starting point to create a straight line. Next, click an ending point while holding down Shift.
    *   Hold down the mouse button while using the Brush tool like an airbrush to build up color without dragging.

Paint tool option

Use the options bar to adjust the following parameters. Be aware that according to the tool that is used, different alternatives may be accessible.

Mode

Selecting a blending mode will affect how your painted color will mix with the surrounding pixels. Depending on which tool is presently used, several modes may be accessible. These paint modes work in a manner akin to layer blending modes.

Opacity

Modifies the applied color's transparency. When you paint over an area, the opacity controls how transparent the color gets. This means that no matter how many strokes you take until you release the mouse button, the color will never go above the specified threshold. Repainting the same area adds additional color in proportion to the opacity that was previously selected. Total opacity is achieved with an opacity of 100%.

Flow

Changes the speed at which color is applied while the cursor is sweeping across an area. The color builds up according to the flow rate when you paint over an area while holding down the mouse button, up to the designated opacity setting. For example, when opacity and flow are both set to 33%, every stroke over an area shifts the color of the brush 33% closer to the original color. Unless the mouse button is released and the region is stroked again, the total opacity will not exceed 33%.

Airbrush

Recreates the paint-building effect of an airbrush by moving the cursor over a surface while depressing the mouse button. The brush opacity, flow parameters, and hardness all affect how quickly and how much paint is applied. Toggle the button to turn on or off the airbrush simulation.

Auto erase

Photoshop's auto-erase feature makes it easier to remove components from a picture by automatically substituting them with the transparency or background color. This function helps you get rid of unwanted items, flaws, or faults in your pictures.

Regions that include the foreground color are replaced with the selected background color using the pencil tool. Choose the color to be substituted in the foreground and the suitable background color. Start a line drawing using your mouse or touchpad. Photoshop creates a line in the active foreground color when you start dragging from a different spot on the page. You may use your mouse or touchpad to click on the regions you want to erase, or you can drag over the desired areas while holding down Alt (Windows) or Option (Mac OS).

Selection in Photoshop

A selection is a specific region inside an image that you mark for editing, allowing you to focus on and isolate particular areas of the image. Increasing the quality of your choices allows you to edit, add effects, and use filters on parts of your picture that you have chosen without affecting the unselected sections.

A multitude of tools, commands, and Photoshop's Select and Mask workspace may be used to create selections. A boundary defines the chosen region once a decision has been made. After that, you can manipulate, copy, or remove any pixels that are inside the selection boundary; however, until the selection is deselected, you cannot modify any regions that are outside of it.

Move, Hide, or invert a selection.

Move a selection

1. Select the Move tool.
2. Place the cursor inside the selection boundary.
3. Drag the option to a different place. When you drag, every region that is chosen will move together.

Copy and paste the selection.

Use the Move tool to duplicate selections while moving them across or within pictures, or to copy and reposition selections. Because it doesn't use the clipboard, this technique saves memory.

A selection or layer that you paste across different resolution photographs keeps its pixel dimensions. Because of this, the pasted area might appear out of proportion to the updated image. To fix this, before copying and pasting, make sure the source and destination photos have the same resolution by using the Image Size command. As an alternative, you can resize the copied information by using the Free Transform command.

Copy a selection

In Photoshop, copying a selection entails identifying the area of the original picture that you wish to replicate. Here is a detailed procedure:

1. **Choose the Area**
   - Outline the area you wish to duplicate using one of the selection tools (such as the Magic Wand, Lasso, or Rectangular Marquee). By doing this, a boundary designating the chosen area is created.
2. **Duplicate the selection**

- Navigate to the "Edit" menu.
- Choose either "Copy" or "Copy Merged" based on your requirements:
  - Copy: This function makes an identical copy of the specified region.
  - Copy Merged: Use this option if you have numerous layers and wish to copy a composite of all the visible layers, including the backdrop.

Copy a selection while dragging.

The Move tool can be activated by selecting it or by holding down the Ctrl (Windows) or Command (Mac OS) key.

Drag the selected area to copy and move it after pressing and holding Alt (Windows) or Option (Mac OS.

Drag the selection from the window with the active picture to the window with the destination image to copy between images. Copying the whole active layer occurs if no particular selection is made. A border highlighting the window will appear when you drag the selection over another image window, letting you drop the selection into it.

Create multiple copies of a selection within an image

Activate the Move tool by selecting it or holding down Ctrl (Win) or Command (Mac).

Copy the selection:

Press and hold Alt (Win) or Option (Mac), then drag the selection.

Using an arrow key and Alt or Option, duplicate the selection and shift it to one pixel.

Use the arrow keys and Alt+Shift (Win) or Option+Shift (Mac) to duplicate the selection and move the duplicate by 10 pixels.

A copy of the selection is created with each arrow keystroke while holding down Alt or Option. The duplicate is offset from the previous one by the preset distance. This case involves creating the clone on the same layer.

Control the movement of a selection.

Start dragging; to restrict the direction to multiples of 45°, hold down Shift while dragging.

Using an arrow key will yield precise 1-pixel steps.

To adjust the selection in 10-pixel increments, hold down Shift while using an arrow key.

Adjust a selection manually.

Apply the selection tools to enhance or reduce the pixel selections that are already in place.

Before adjusting a selection by hand, think about matching the feather and anti-aliasing settings in the options bar to the ones used in the original selection.

Add to a selection or select an additional area

Make a decision.

Perform one of the following actions using any selecting tool:

Choose "Add to Selection" from the options bar and drag more items to increase the size of the selection.

Drag more items into the selection by selecting the "Add to Selection" option from the options bar.

The cursor will have a + sign next to it to indicate that you are extending the selection.

Subtract from a selection.

The tool you need to use to subtract from a selection is called Subtract from Selection. It can be found in the toolbar on the left side of the screen. Additionally, you may activate it by using the keyboard commands Alt on Windows or Option on Mac OS. You may exclude chosen regions from the selection by painting them in black or white using the Subtract from Selection tool.

One of the following can be done with any selection tool:

- Click the Subtract from Selection option in the options box, then drag to join other choices.
- While dragging, hold down Alt (Windows) or Option (Mac OS) to remove a selection.
- A negative symbol appears next to the cursor when you subtract from a selection.

Create a selection around a selection border.

Choose a width of pixels within and outside an existing selection border by using the Border command. This comes in handy when you have to choose a band of pixels or border around an area of an image instead of the area itself, such as when you're cleaning up a halo effect around a pasted item.

Observe these actions:

1. Make your first selection using a selection tool.

2. Proceed to Choose > Adjust > Border.

3. Click OK after entering a number for the new selection's border width, which should range from 1 to 200 pixels.

The final selection, which is centered within the first selection boundary, frames the initial picked region. A 20-pixel border, for example, creates a new, gently edged selection that is 10 pixels within and 10 pixels outside of the old selection boundary.

Expand a selection to include areas with similar colors

Extending a selection to encompass regions with corresponding hues, perform one of the following actions:

Select > Expand to include all surrounding pixels within the tolerance range of the Magic Wand.

To incorporate all pixels within the tolerance range in the picture, not just those that are adjacent to one another, choose Select > Similar.

Remove fringe pixels from a selection.

When anti-aliased selections are moved or pasted, a fringe or halo appears around the pasted selection's edges because some pixels surrounding the selection boundary are included. There are options for improving the quality of unwanted edge pixels using the Layer > Matting commands:

- **Color Decontaminate:** Substitutes background colors in fringe pixels with the color of fully selected pixels nearby.

256

- **Defringe:** Changes the color of pixels that are closer to the selection's edge but do not have a background color to the color of pixels that are fringed.
- **Remove Black Matte and Remove White Matte:** These functions come in handy when you need to paste a selection that has been anti-aliased against a white or black backdrop onto a different background. For example, gray pixels around the borders of black text that have been anti-aliased on a white backdrop may show up against a colorful background.

Decrease fringe on a selection.

Select Layer > Matting > Defringe.
Input a value in the width box to define the area for locating replacement pixels. Typically, a distance of 1 or 2 pixels is sufficient. Click OK.

How to use colors in the foreground and Background

Color is vital to design because it enhances the overall visual appeal of the work, produces contrast, and gives an image life. Artists may finely manipulate the color scheme that shapes a picture by using Photoshop to select the colors for the background and foreground. This enhances the aesthetic appeal while also simplifying color manipulation.

Photoshop's background color is used for gradient fills and filling in erased portions of a picture, while the foreground color is utilized for selection painting, filling, and stroking. Certain special effects filters also make use of the foreground and backdrop colors.

To change the foreground or background color, you may use tools like the Adobe Color Picker, Color panel, Eyedropper tool, and Swatches panel.

White is the background color by default, and black is the foreground color. (In an alpha channel, white and black represent the basic foreground and background colors).

The basic concept of this tool is straightforward. Whereas the backdrop color acts as an eraser, removing any color that has been applied and substituting it with the default white background color, the foreground determines the color of your brush or pencil. However, when erasing on a transparent layer, the erased region becomes transparent. If you opt to enlarge your canvas, the background color covers the additional area. The backdrop color has an impact on the gradients you make as well.

Choose colors in the Tool Box.

The toolbox presents the current background color in the bottom box and the current foreground color in the upper color selection box.

The toolbox's foreground and background color boxes:

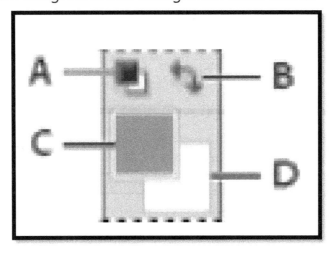

A symbol indicating the default color scheme B. The sign for the Colors Switch C. The color box in the foreground D. The background color box

- Select the upper color selection box from the toolbox and utilize the Adobe Color Picker to choose a color to alter the foreground color.
- Select a color from the Adobe Color Picker by clicking the toolbox's lower color selection box to change the backdrop color.
- To change the backdrop and foreground colors, click the Switch Colors icon in the Toolbox.
- The regular foreground and background colors can be restored by clicking the Default Colors button.

Choose colors with the Eyedropper Tool.

Use the Eyedropper tool to sample colors to select a new background or foreground color. Any region of the screen, including the current picture, may be used to collect samples.

Take these actions:

1. Choose the tool called Eyedropper.

2. Select the desired sample size for the eyedropper from the Sample Size menu in the options bar:

Point Sample: The value of the clicked pixel is accurately determined.

3. Select one of the following options from the Sample menu:

- **All Layers**: Provides color samples from every document layer.
- **Current Layer:** Color samples taken from the layer that is currently active.

4. Turn on the "Show Sampling Ring" option to surround the Eyedropper tool with a ring that shows a sampled color over the foreground color that is now selected.

5. Choose one of the following actions:

- To select a different foreground color, click anywhere within the image. As an alternative, move the cursor over the picture, click, and drag it anywhere on the screen. As you drag, the selection box for the foreground color changes dynamically. To verify the new color, let go of the mouse button.

- Use the Alt- or Option-click keys within the image to change the background color on Windows or Mac OS. Another way is to put the pointer over the picture, hit Alt on Windows or Options on Mac OS, then hit the mouse button and drag the cursor wherever on the screen. You may drag to see the selection box's dynamic background color changing. When you select a new color, let go of the mouse.

NB: Apply the Eyedropper tool with the Alt (Windows) or Option (Mac OS) key down to temporarily choose a foreground color while using any painting tool.

Adobe Color Picker Overview

The Adobe Color Picker offers you four color models: HSB, RGB, Lab, and CMYK. This tool allows you to select the text, background, and foreground colors as well as the target colors for various commands, tools, and options.

You may choose colors from established color schemes or merely the web-safe palette using the Adobe Color Picker's setup settings. There is now a high dynamic range (HDR) picker available to select colors in HDR images.

The HSB, RGB, and Lab color modes are used to show color components in the Color field of the Adobe Color Picker. If you know the precise color value, you may enter it in text areas. Utilize the color slider and field to examine and select a color. Whenever these tools are used to adjust the color, the numerical values are updated dynamically. The color box adjacent to the slider displays the altered color in the top portion, while the original color is presented in the bottom section. An alarm will sound (non-printable) if a color is not within the print gamut or is not web-safe.)

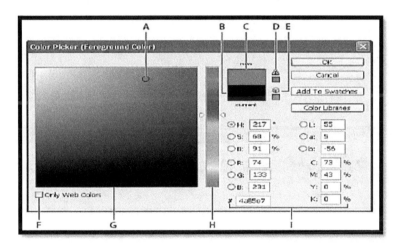

A. Color selection B. The first hue C. Modified the color D. A warning indicator for out-of-gamut E. A warning symbol for non-web-safe colors F. Only uses web-safe color schemes. G. Field of color H. The color divider I. Values of color.

NB: The hexadecimal, CMYK, RGB, Lab, and HSB numerical values are displayed simultaneously in the Adobe Color Picker while you are choosing a color. This is useful for comprehending how several color models represent a given color.

Even though Photoshop uses the Adobe Color Picker by default, you may use another one by changing your options. For example, you may use the color picker that is pre-installed with your computer's operating system or you can incorporate a color picker that is a third-party plug-in.

How to Edit Text

1. Open the Photoshop file containing the text you wish to edit.
2. Click on the Type tool in the toolbar.
3. Make sure the text you wish to alter is visible.
4. To modify the font size, color, typeface, alignment, and style, utilize the options bar at the top.

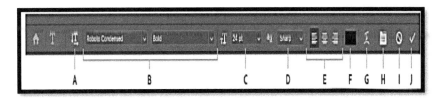

The following options are accessible on macOS in the Photoshop Options Bar:

A. Change the text orientation from vertical to horizontal B. Modify the font style C. Change the font size D. Regulate the pixelation of the text edges (anti-aliasing) E. Adjust the text's alignment F. Adjust text color G. Apply text warping H. Seek for other settings in the Character and Paragraph panels I. Reverse any modifications J. Save the made adjustments.

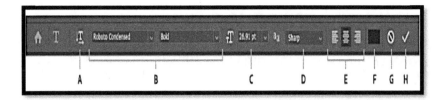

Options accessible on Windows in the Photoshop Options Bar:
A. Easily switch between text orientations (horizontal and vertical); B. Customize font style; C. Change font size; D. Manage text edge pixelation (anti-aliasing). E. Change the location of the text F. Change the color of the text; G. Undo any modifications; H. Save the made adjustments

For further text editing options, you may also use the Character and Paragraph panels.

5. Finally, click on the options bar to save your changes.

Specify curly or straight quotes.

Curly quotes, sometimes known as smart quotes, are quotation marks that slant slightly toward the text they encircle. These quotes are more aesthetically pleasing and provide clarity than straight quotes, which lack directionality and curvature. The quotation marks at the beginning and end of each quote seem to be the same and indistinguishable from one another.

Use keyboard shortcuts Shift+Ctrl+[and Shift+Ctrl+] (or their Mac counterparts) for straight double quotes and Ctrl+[and Ctrl+] for straight single quotes. Make changes to these shortcuts by using the keyboard shortcut editor.

Alternatively, choose "Use smart quotes" from the list of options by going to Edit > Preferences > Type & Character > Typewriter & Symbols. This will automatically insert curly quotation marks into your text.

Apply anti-aliasing to a type layer.

Anti-aliasing is a technique that blends text and graphic edges with the backdrop color to improve their smoothness. When working with complicated forms or high-resolution photos, this approach is extremely helpful for generating a more polished and natural appearance.

The Text tool may be selected from the toolbar or made active by using the "T" key on your keyboard. You may select an already-existing text layer or create a new one by clicking on the canvas. Find the Options bar at the top of the screen and navigate to the "Anti-Aliasing" dropdown option. Based on personal choice, choose from smooth, crisp, strong, or sharp anti-aliasing.

Check and Correct Spelling

At this point, you can spell-check a document, a narrative, a sample of text, or all open documents. Spell checking reveals misspelled words, duplicate text, and capitalization errors. Additionally, dynamic spelling allows you to see potential mistakes highlighted in real time as you type.

Adding new phrases is an easy process, and the spell-check process uses the dictionary of the specified language.

1. Select Spelling Check from the Edit menu.

- Word processing begins with a spell check.

2. Use the Search dropdown menu to choose the appropriate search range::

- All Documents: Search for all available papers.
- Document: Scans of the chosen document.

- Story: Analyzes the chosen frame, including text that is overset and included in other threaded text frames.
- To End of Story: This search runs from the story's selection point to its conclusion.
- Selection: Only checks the text that has been chosen for mistakes. This option can only be accessed when text is chosen.

3. Select "Start."

4. Select a word from the list of suggested corrections or manually enter the term in the Change To field. After that, choose "Change" or "Change All" to change the text that is highlighted.

Alternatively, select "Skip" or "Ignore All" to proceed without altering the highlighted text".

Find and Replace Text

When working together on a document that is being revised often, using the "find and replace" panel may greatly increase productivity. Across several open documents or inside a single document, you may use this functionality to find and change specific content.

It is possible to look for and edit plain and formatted text within an InDesign document as well as between documents. Are you trying to find text that has a certain formatting property?

1. Navigate to Edit > Find/Change.

2. Select the Text tab and type the text you want to search for in the Find What field.

Leave the Find What and Change To fields Blank to locate and replace certain format attributes.

3. Click on the Specify attributes to find the icon in the Find Format section.

4. Select a formatting type, specify the format parameters, and click OK to close the Find Format Settings box.

5. Click on the Specify attributes to change icon in the Change Format section. Then, choose a formatting type, define the format attributes, and click OK.

6. Click on Find Next.

To change the located text, choose Change, Change All, or Change/Find.

Assign a language for Text.

Open Photoshop, select Edit > Options> General (Windows) or Photoshop > Preferences > General (Mac) to change your language options. Choose the Interface Menu from the Preferences panel, then change the UI Language settings to the language of your choice.

Step 1: Open the Preferences Window Go to Edit > Preferences > General (Windows) or Photoshop > Preferences > General (Mac) after launching Photoshop.

Step 2: Open the Preferences window, navigate to the Interface Tab, and choose Interface from the left-hand panel.

Step 3: Go to Presentation in the Interface window, select Presentation from the dropdown menu, and change the UI Language to the language of your choice.

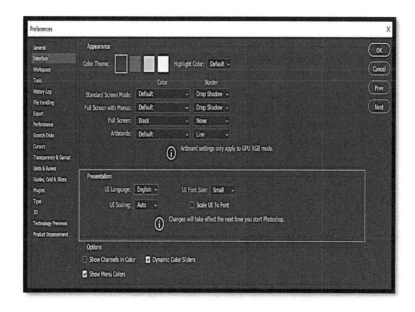

Adjust the Scale of Type

Text may be resized easily in Photoshop using a few different efficient techniques. These are the best methods to use in Photoshop when scaling text.

Text Scaling Using Free Transform: Using the Free Transform Tool is the fastest way to scale text. All you have to do is press V to choose the Move Tool and drag the transform box outward from any corner. The font size will automatically adapt proportionately as you scale the content.

Rotate Type

There are two easy ways to rotate text in Photoshop, and based on the desired angle, each has a different purpose. Let's look at these options and compare and contrast their text rotation capabilities.

Using Free Transform to Rotate A Photo

Free Transform is an easy-to-use tool for rotating text. With this option, you may use your mouse to click and drag the text to change its direction.

   1. Select your text layer, then click Edit > Free Transform or press V to open the Move Tool.

2. Hover your cursor over any corner of your text to see a U-shaped arrow with two sides emerge.

3. To rotate the text to the appropriate orientation, click and drag with your mouse. To achieve a certain angle, use the angle box that shows as a guide.

4. If you have a precise angle in mind, you can type it in the settings bar. Simply enter the desired angle and press Enter.

Rotating Text by 90 Degrees

Manual rotation might not be the most effective way if you know you want to rotate your text by a perfect ninety degrees. One-click will speed up the procedure if you rotate your text.

1. Choose Edit > Transform > Rotate 90 Clockwise or Rotate 90 Counter Clockwise while your text layer is chosen.

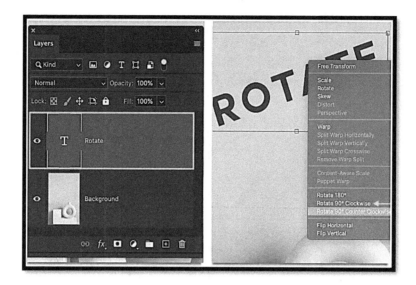

2. As an alternative, when using Free Transform, you may right-click on your text to obtain comparable rotation options.

Rotate vertical characters

The letters in Photoshop will never line up vertically, no matter how many times you try to rotate the text. There's a quick fix in Photoshop to create vertical lettering without having to rotate each letter separately.

Find the Toggle Text Orientation button in the options bar while your text is chosen and the Text Tool is active. It's right next to the font selections.

This button will cause your text to instantaneously change from horizontal to vertical orientation when you click on it.

Change the orientation of a type of Layer.

The orientation of a type layer determines the direction of type lines concerning the bounding box (paragraph type) or the document window (point type). In a vertical type layer, the type flows up and down, while in a horizontal type layer, it flows from left to right. It is important to differentiate the direction of the characters inside a type line from the orientation of a type layer.

1. From the Layers panel, choose the type layer.

2. Execute any of the subsequent steps:

- Select a typing tool and tap the settings bar's Text Orientation button.
- Select either Layer > Type > Vertical or Layer > Type > Horizontal.
- From the Character panel menu, select Change Text Orientation.

Rasterize Type Layers

Type layers cannot be directly affected by some commands or tools, such as painting tools and filter effects. The type layer must be rasterized to be used with these tools. Rasterizing makes the text inside the type layer uneditable and turns it into a regular layer. If you try to use a tool or command that needs a rasterized layer, a warning notice will show up. A button labeled "OK" might occasionally appear in the warning message, enabling you to rasterize the layer.

Selecting a type layer and choosing Layer > Rasterize > Type will rasterize it.

How to add or Place text

1. Launch a Photoshop file or picture.

2. Use the toolbar to access the Type tool by either clicking on the icon or hitting 'T.' You may add text horizontally by using the Horizontal Type Tool, which is the default setting. Click the Type tool once more and select the Vertical Type Tool from the context menu if you would rather add text vertically.

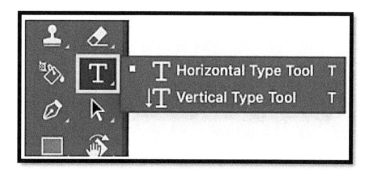

3. Do you wish to insert a brief text, such as a heading or title? Click on any location on the canvas to input it. In Photoshop, this is referred to as point text.

Alternatively, utilize the paragraph text option if you plan to compose a paragraph. You may create a bounding box that will allow you to insert your paragraph by clicking and dragging the mouse over the canvas. This method makes it easier to alter and align the paragraph content in the future.

NB: A type layer, denoted by the T symbol in the Layers panel, is automatically produced when you generate point or paragraph text.

4. Enter your text. To preserve your modifications, select in the options bar or press Esc, and you're all set!

The macOS options bar in Photoshop.

The Windows options bar in Photoshop.

How to Select Text

1. Open the Photoshop document containing the text you wish to edit.
2. Double-click on the appropriate text to highlight the entire paragraph or text on a type layer by activating the Move tool from the toolbar.
3. To pick one or more characters on a type layer, just select the Type tool from the toolbar, then move the pointer over the desired characters.

Draw and edit shapes.

Photoshop shape generation and alteration is a creative and entertaining way to work on your photographs. With the help of the shape tools, you can create unique forms or choices and add different features like colors, patterns, photos, and other aspects to them.

Create shapes

Here's a quick tutorial on using Photoshop to create shapes:

1. Choose a shape Tool

Click and hold the Shape tool group icon from the toolbar to access the Shape tool choices, which include Rectangle, Ellipse, Triangle,

Polygon, Line, and Custom Shape. Choose the right tool for the shape you wish to sketch.

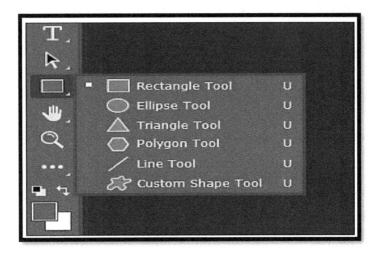

2. Set Up Shape Tool Parameters

The following parameters are adjustable using the shape tool options bar:

- **Mode:** Select a shape tool mode from the available options: Shape, Path, and Pixels.
- **Fill:** To fill your shape, choose a color.
- **Stroke**: Select the kind, color, and width of the stroke on your object.
- **W&H:** Adjust the shape's height and width manually.
- **Path Operations:** Use path operations to ascertain the relationships between your forms.
- **Path Alignment**: Make use of path alignment to distribute and align the parts of your form.
- **Path Arrangement:** Set the stacking order of the shapes you create with path arrangement.

- **Extra Shape and route choices:** To access additional shape and route choices, click the gear () symbol. With the help of these settings, you may restrict options when creating shapes and change the path's width and color on the screen.

3. Create a Shape

Click and drag on the canvas using your chosen shape tool to draw a shape. This action automatically generates a new shape layer in the Layers panel.

While sketching, hold down the Shift key to make sure your shapes stay proportionate. Use the Move tool to change your shape's location on the canvas while your shape layer is chosen. To easily scale, transform, or rotate your shape, select Edit > Free transform or use Control+T on a Windows or Command+T on a Mac

4. Modify the Shape's Properties

It's simple to change the properties of your shapes using the on-canvas tools directly or by going to Shape Properties in the Properties panel. On-canvas controls improve the intuitiveness of your interactions with forms.

Utilize the canvas's rounding and transform features to improve the appearance of your shape. On-canvas transform controls are compatible with keyboard modifiers in the same manner as Photoshop's Transform tool. To modify the radius of a single corner, drag it, or press Alt (for Windows) or Option (for Mac) to modify the radius of all corners simultaneously. When one corner of a triangle is altered, the other corners will follow suit. It's easy to rotate a form with the on-canvas rotate handle, which appears when you hover over your item on the canvas.

To reverse any changes at any time, click the reset symbol in the Properties window.

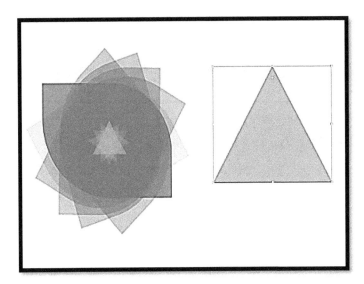

Once you have drawn a shape, you may modify its parameters by clicking anywhere on the canvas to trigger the Create Shape pop-up window.

Sketch a Unique Shape

Use the forms in the Custom Shape pop-up Panel to create custom shapes, or store a route or shape to be used as a custom shape at a later time.

1. **Select the Custom Shape Tool**: From the shape tools in the toolbar, select the Custom Shape tool.

2. **Access Custom Shapes**: Click the gear icon located to the right of the Custom Shape choice in the shape tool options bar to access all of the custom shapes that come with Photoshop. You may

choose your preferred custom shape from the list of forms that will be displayed as a result of this operation.

3. **Import or Create Custom Shapes**: To import a shape from your saved files, click the gear icon in the Custom Shape picker box if you are unable to locate the appropriate form. Additionally, you may make and store a custom shape in your library.

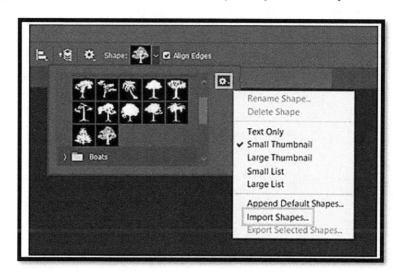

4. Simply modify the Custom Shape Tool's features from inside Shape features in the Properties panel. Additionally, you may alter a custom shape while maintaining its original attributes by using the on-canvas transform controls. To design your unique shape, just click and drag anywhere on the canvas.

Additionally, the Shapes panel gives you the ability to specify Custom Shape Tool settings directly. This preset in the Custom Shape Tool > Custom Shape picker will automatically change when you select a custom shape from Windows > Shape panel.

NB: After a route has been transformed into a shape, custom shape characteristics are not accessible for shapes created with the Custom Shape Tool.

Save a shape or path as a custom shape.

1. Select a path from the Paths panel. A vector mask for a form layer, a work path, or a saved path can all be used as routes.

2. Select Edit > Define Custom Shape. Give the new custom shape a name in the Shape Name dialog box. The freshly created shape is now visible in the Shape pop-up panel that is accessible through the options bar.

3. To store the newly formed custom shape as a component of a new library, choose store Shapes from the pop-up panel menu.

Accessing legacy custom shapes

Use these procedures to import Legacy Custom Shapes that you used in previous Photoshop versions into the one you're using now:

Select Window from the main window to access Shapes.

Select Legacy Shapes and More after clicking the menu icon in the Shapes panel's top right corner.

How to add texture to a photo

Photoshop requires a main photo and a texture image to add texture. As scaling is feasible, the texture file's size difference from the primary picture is negligible. The primary picture should ideally not be too detailed, allowing some surrounding area for textures to improve the image's aesthetic appeal.

Step 1: Open Images in Photoshop Open both your main image and the texture image in Photoshop. Select both image files and choose Photo > Edit In > Open as Layers in Photoshop. This action will open a single Photoshop document with two layers—one for your main image and the other for the texture.

Change the texture layer's name to "Texture" and make sure the Layers panel places it above your main image.

Select Windows > Layers from the Windows drop-down menu if the Layers panel isn't visible in the workspace.

Open your primary image first in Photoshop if you're opening files straight from there. Using the new layer icon at the bottom of the Layers panel or selecting Layer > New > Layer will allow you to create a new, blank layer. Click OK after renaming this layer to "Texture". Photoshop will replicate the texture file you drag onto the empty layer. Resizing the texture layer to make it fit over your picture layer is the next step.

Step 2: Adjust Texture Layer Size Navigate to the Edit menu after selecting the texture layer. Press Ctrl or Cmd+T to choose Edit > Free Transform. Once the texture completely encloses your picture layer, drag its corners and edges. You may separately alter each edge by holding down the Shift key and dragging. Press Return or Enter, or click the checkmark located at the top of the workspace.

Experiment with rotating the texture layer for different effects. Go to Edit > Transform > Rotate 90° Clockwise or use Free Transform to rotate the image.

Adjust the texture layer's size until it completely engulfs the main image. Next, you will want to show your primary photo by blending the layers.

Step 3: Adjust the Blending Parameter Layer interaction is determined by the blend modes used. They are in the Normal mode by default and may be found close to the top of the Layers panel.

Lighten, Overlay, and Soft Light are popular blend modes for applying textures. Explore the variations in your image by clicking on each mix mode. While several settings modify colors, others let more of your primary image be seen.

As there is no strict rule, choose a blending option that you enjoy. Reducing the amount of texture that is visible is the next phase.

Step 4: Improve the Texture Overlay Just where you want it to show through, fine-tune the texture overlay. Generally speaking, you want the texture to accentuate the focal picture without overpowering it.

Reduce the texture layer's opacity first. The Opacity slider at the top of the Layers panel may be adjusted by clicking on the texture layer. There is no default opacity level; try 50%, for example, and adjust until the proper balance is reached.

It is also possible to reduce or eliminate the texture in certain areas of your primary image. By selecting Layer > Layer Mask > Reveal All after clicking on the texture layer, you may create a layer mask. As an alternative, select the Layers panel's layer mask icon at the bottom. It looks like a circle inside a rectangle.

Next to your texture, you'll notice a white rectangle; choose the white layer mask. Choose the Paintbrush tool, adjust the opacity to 40–50%, and apply a gentle brush. Overpaint the areas where you wish to soften or eliminate the texture.

Observe that the texture is hidden by black on the layer mask and revealed by white. If you make a mistake, you may restore the texture by using a white paintbrush. Certain sections can be delicately made lighter or darker by using a low-opacity brush.

CHAPTER TEN

USING THE SPOT HEALING TOOL

Spot Healing Brush: This tool effectively removes blemishes and other flaws from your images. Selecting pixels from an image or pattern functions similarly to the Healing Brush, matching texture, lighting, transparency, and shading with the pixels that require repair.

Interestingly, you don't even need to select a sample point when using the spot Healing Brush—it just takes a sample from around the retouched area.

NB: If you want greater control over source sampling or need to retouch a big area, use the Healing Brush instead of the Spot Healing Brush.

1. Choose the Spot Healing Brush tool from the toolbar. To access the secret tools and make your choice, choose the Red Eye, Patch, or Healing Brush tools as necessary.

2. In the settings bar, select the brush size. Employing a brush that is somewhat bigger than the desired region should be your goal to guarantee that you may apply one click to the full area.

3. (Optional) Select a blending mode using the settings bar's Mode menu. When using a soft edge brush, choose "Replace" to maintain texture, noise, and film grain at the brush stroke's edges.

4. **Choose a Type option in the options bar**:

    • Proximity Match: Locates a patchable region by using pixels surrounding the selection's boundary.

- Create Texture: This function creates a texture by using the pixels in the selection. If you're not happy with the texture, try dragging through the region again.
- Content-Aware: This technique smoothly fills the selection with relevant information like shadows and object edges by comparing it to neighboring picture content.

5. Choose "Sample All Layers" from the options bar to take a sample of the data from each visible layer. Uncheck "Sample All Layers" if you want to sample solely from the current layer.

6. Click and drag, or click on the area you want to fix, to cover up problems in a wider area.

Healing Brush Tool

Any flaws may be made to vanish and fit in with the surroundings by using the Healing Brush tool. Similar to cloning tools, use the Healing Brush tool to paint using sampled pixels from an image or pattern.

Nevertheless, this program goes beyond basic reproduction by matching the sampled pixels' texture, lighting, transparency, and coloring to the repaired pixels.

Consequently, it is impossible to differentiate the restored pixels from the original. Animation or video frames can be used with the Healing Brush tool.

For hints and examples on how to use this tool, see Examples for the Healing Brush in Photoshop.

To use the Healing Brush tool:

1. Choose the Healing Brush tool.

2. In the pop-up box that appears, click the brush sample in the options bar to modify the brush settings.

   - **Mode:** Indicates the blending technique. If you are using a soft-edge brush, choose "Replace" to keep the noise, texture, and film grain at the brush stroke's edges.

   - **Source**: Identify the source of pixel repair. Select "Pattern" to utilize pixels from a pattern, or "Sampled" to use pixels from the currently shown picture. When you choose "Pattern," choose a design from the Pattern pop-up menu.

   - **Aligned:** When enabled, even if you let go of the mouse button, the chosen pixels will continue to be sampled without losing the current sampling point. Every time you stop and start painting again, deselect "Aligned" to keep utilizing the sampled pixels from the first sampling point.

   - **Sample:** Takes data samples from the designated layers. Select "Current and Below" to sample from both the visible levels below the current layer. Select "Current Layer" to just take a sample from the active layer. Select "All Layers" to sample all visible layers. Select "All Layers" and utilize the "Ignore

Adjustment Layers" option located to the right of the Sample pop-up menu to take a sample from every visible layer aside from the adjustment layers.

- **Diffusion**: Sets the speed at which the pasted area resizes to fit the surrounding picture. For photographs with fine details or grain, use a lower number; for smoother images, choose a higher value.

3. To determine the sampling point, move the pointer over a section of the image and use the Alt or Option keys to click (on Windows or macOS), respectively.

NB: If one picture is in grayscale mode, then both images must be in the same color mode when taking a sample from one and applying it to another.

4. Select a clone source button and specify an extra sample point in the Clone Source screen. You can set up to five different sample sources (optional). Until you close the document you are editing, the sampled sources are kept in the Clone Source panel

5. Use the clone source button in the Clone Source tab to choose the desired sampled source. (Details optional)

6. (Optional) In the Clone Source panel, carry out any of the following operations:

- You can input a value for W (width), H (height), or the rotation in degrees to scale or rotate the source that you're copying.

7. Drag within the image.

Every time the mouse button is released, the sampled pixels merge perfectly with the original pixels.

Retouch with Remove Tool

The Remove tool uses cutting-edge technology to fill in the backdrop automatically when users brush over unwanted things. It keeps objects' integrity intact and keeps depth in complex and varied backgrounds. This skill is particularly effective for moving bigger things while maintaining the borders between them.

One example of how the tool maintains the realism of the hilly terrain in an image of a scene is that it may remove a full structure or automobile.

To substitute undesired elements in your image using the Remove tool, follow these steps:

1. Select the tool labeled Remove from the set.

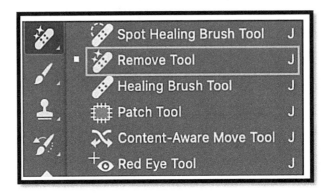

NB: A dialog box that requests the automated installation of necessary components can appear when you use the tool for the first time.

2. Choose your brush size by using the Size field in the options bar. Make sure the brush size is somewhat bigger than the target area to get complete coverage of the whole region in a single stroke.

3. (Optional) Press the Pressure for Size button to allow stylus pressure to be used to change the brush size.

4. (Optional) To sample data from all visible layers, activate Sample All Layers in the settings box.

NB: You may create and choose a new layer, then enable Sample All Layers for a non-destructive procedure. In this manner, fresh pixels will be produced on the layer that is now chosen.

5. (Optional) to permit several brush strokes before applying the fill, disable Remove after each stroke. This works well for complex or huge regions. To apply the fill right away after finishing a stroke, enable Remove after each stroke.

6. Apply a gentle swipe motion to any desired spot that has to go. Click Apply in the options bar to carry out the removal if Remove after each stroke is disabled.

NB: To improve stability if you experience any problems with the Remove tool, go to Preferences > Image Processing > Remove Tool Processing and choose More Stable.

Recommended/Minimum Hardware Environment for Remove Tool

Windows Users

Minimum hardware requirements:

- Processor: Eight cores (Intel Rocket Lake CPU or a similar type).

- GPU: A discrete GPU card with at least 8 GB of RAM, such as an NVidia RTX 3060 or higher

- Memory: 16 GB

- SSD Storage: 512 GB

MacOS Users

Minimum hardware requirements:

- Eight cores on the CPU

- Memory: 16 GB

- GPU: Mid-range discrete GPU card with at least 8 GB of RAM

- 512 GB of SSD storage

- The OS version is 12.6.3

- Processor: Intel comparable or M1 Pro ARM

Known issues with the remove Tool and its workarounds

Some components must be downloaded from Adobe servers to use the Remove tool. This download begins automatically when Photoshop is installed using Creative Cloud Desktop. Once everything is complete, click the three dots next to Photoshop's Open button and choose Add-ons to verify that the Remove tool components have been installed.

It's possible to launch Photoshop before the installation is finished. However, be aware that using the Remove tool might cause the issues listed below.

Issue and Resolution

Crash on using the Remove tool.

Update your GPU drivers if you get a crash when trying to utilize the Remove tool. To further enhance stability, choose Preferences > Image Processing > Remove Tool Processing > More Stable.
The message "Required components are being downloaded" appears on the screen. Once the download is finished, come back later to utilize the tool."
When selecting the Remove tool, a dialog box may appear to indicate that the download is in progress. The components only need to be downloaded once. Do not cancel the download and choose to go back to the previous tool.

There was an error downloading the components" is the error message that appears.

This issue could show up while components are being downloaded from the Adobe server.

Ensure that your computer is connected to the Internet. Free up disk space, as the feature components require 0.5 GB to 1 GB of disk space. Then, re-select the Remove tool. Restart Photoshop and re-select the Remove tool.

New interactions in remove tool

When removing an area, create a loop around it with the Remove tool rather than brushing over it entirely. Interestingly, Photoshop will determine how far apart to connect the loop and fill it in automatically, saving you from really having to close it.

Large sections may now be selected without having to erase the entire area, which simplifies the removal process. Consequently, when sweeping over a broad region to be deleted, there is a lower likelihood of missing pixels, which produces more desirable results.

Follow these steps to create a closed loop around the element you want to eliminate:

1. Use a brush to clean the area's perimeter. The endpoints don't need to be completely linked.
2. Everything that falls inside the loop and beneath the brush will be eliminated. By using object detection, this interaction refines the region.
3. Raise the mouse or pen, or, if multi-stroke is enabled, click the apply (checkmark) button in the options bar.
4. Check out the automated filling of the overlay area.

Tip: This interaction may be used with the multi-stroke checkbox (Remove after each stroke) selected or unchecked. To remedy inadvertent selections made while surrounding an item, switch the brush stroke mode from addition to subtraction.

Follow these steps to understand how to use the addition (+) and subtraction (–) modes:

1. To activate multiple stroke mode, uncheck the Remove option located in the Tool Options Bar after each stroke.

2. Draw a brush stroke to indicate the removal region.

3. To switch to the subtraction mode, click the subtraction mode (–) button in the tool options bar.

4. Brush again on the image to subtract specific parts from the highlighted area.

5. Continue to brush to further refine the region that has to be eliminated, and switch between the (+) and (-) modes as needed.

6. Once you've completed refining, hit the apply checkbox or hit Enter to start the process of removing every item in the highlighted area.

Tip: Use the keyboard shortcuts for the Option (on Mac) and Alt (on Windows) to quickly and momentarily switch between the addition (+) and subtraction (–) modes.

How to use the Clone stamp tool

Painting one area of a picture over another or any open document in the same color mode is possible with the Clone Stamp tool. You may also paint over a layer by painting over certain areas of it. Object duplication and picture flaw removal are two applications of this technology. Paint functionality for video or animation frames may also be applied to it.

- If you wish to reproduce (clone) pixels from an area, paint over it and then establish a sample point there using the Clone Stamp tool.
- Use the Aligned option to paint using the most current sampling point each time you pause and restart painting.
- Select the Aligned option to start from the initial sample point regardless of how many times you stop and start painting.

Several brush tips are supported by the Clone Stamp tool, which lets you precisely control the size of the clone area. Furthermore, the opacity and flow parameters allow you to choose how paint is applied to the copied region.

1. Select the toolbar's Clone Stamp option.

2. Choose a suitable brush tip and adjust brush features, such as flow, opacity, and blending mode, in the settings bar.

3. Use the options bar to change the following settings to specify how you want to align the sampled pixels and sample data from the layers in your document:

- **Aligned:** Constantly samples pixels; even when the mouse button is released, the current sampling point is maintained. Every time you pause and begin painting, deselect Aligned to force the application of the sampled pixels from the original sampling point.
- **Sample:** Takes a representative sample of data from the designated layers. To sample from the active layer and any visible layers behind it, select "Current and Below". Select "Current Layer" to take samples just from the active layer. To take a sample from every visible layer, choose "All Layers". Select "All Layers" and select the Ignore Adjustment Layers

button located to the right of the Sample pop-up menu to take a sample from every visible layer, ignoring adjustment layers.

4. Select any open image with the pointer above it, then Alt- or Option-click (Windows) to set the sampling point (macOS).

NB: Ensure that you are not operating on an adjustment layer, as the Clone Stamp tool is not functional on adjustment layers.

5. (Optional) Use the clone source button in the Clone Source tab to select an extra sample point.

You can set up as many as five different sample sources. Until you close the document, the sampled sources are kept in the Clone Source panel.

6. Drag over the specific area of the image that requires correction.

Set sample sources for cloning and healing.

Photoshop's Clone Stamp and Healing Brush tools let you sample sources from inside the active project or from any open document. When working with animation or video, you may pick sources from a different frame, even if it is part of an open document or a distinct video layer, or you can create sample points within the frame you're editing at the moment. In the Clone Source panel, you may simultaneously configure up to five separate sample sources. These sources are still visible in the panel until you close the document.

Follow these steps to set sample sources for cloning and healing

1 Open the Animation panel to clone video or animation frames (if you are not dealing with video or animation frames, move on to step 2). Select the timeline animation option, then align the current-time indication with the frame that contains the source you want to sample.

2. Next, to establish the sampling point, use the Clone Stamp tool and Alt-click (Windows) or Option-click (macOS) in any open document window.

3. The Clone Source panel has many Clone Source buttons that you can use to specify extra sample locations.

Recall that you may change the sampling point by choosing a different Clone Source button, giving you more freedom.

Specify the clone source offset.

Whether you are using the Clone Stamp or Healing Brush tools, you may freely paint over the target picture with the source sample. You may paint at a specific location regarding the sample point by specifying the x and y pixel offset, even though overlay settings allow you to view the painting area.

Open the Clone Source panel, choose your favorite source, and then input the x and y pixel values for the Offset option to fine-tune the painting's placement.

Exporting in Photoshop

The act of storing your work in Photoshop in several sizes and formats for online, print, or video uses is known as exporting. Depending on your requirements and tastes, Photoshop offers a variety of export options.

Quick export As

Use the Quick Export As function to rapidly export your project with the preset parameters that are available in the Quick Export settings.

The Quick Export As option can be accessed using any of the following methods:

- Select [format for picture] under File > Export > Quick Export.
- The Layers panel allows you to choose the layers, layer groups, or artboards you wish to export. Right-click on your selection, then select Quick Export As [image format] from the context menu.

Quick Export Preferences

The format, location, metadata, and color space options for Quick Export can be altered using any of the following methods:

- Take note of the menu and choose Edit > Preferences > Export.
- Navigate to File > Export Preferences and choose Export.

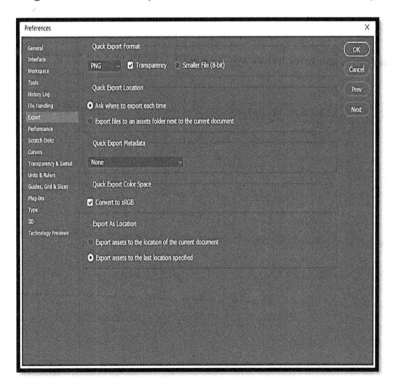

Quick Export preferences for the format, Location Metadata, and color space

The Preferences dialog box allows you to change the following settings:

1. **Quick Export Format:** Select from PNG, JPG, or GIF as the export format for image files. There are more parameters unique to the format accessible. For example, you may choose to have lesser file sizes (8-bit) or to define transparency preferences (32-bit) when using PNG. You may change the output quality for JPG files.

2. **Quick Export Location:** Choose one of the following:
    *   Ask where to export each time: When you export assets, this feature asks you to select a place.
    *   Export data to a folder called assets adjacent to the open document: This locates the picture asset inside the folder holding the original Photoshop document, in a subdirectory called Assets.

3. **Quick Export Metadata:** Make use of this feature to add contact details and copyright information to the exported materials.

4. **Quick Export Color Space:** Choose if you wish to change the assets' color space to sRGB.

Export as dialog configuration

The Export As dialog box allows you to set up the following options:

1. Format: Choose from GIF, JPG, and PNG.
2. Specific parameters for a format:
    *   For PNG, choose whether to export assets with 32-bit transparency enabled or choose to use 8-bit pictures instead.

- For JPEG, move the slider to change the image quality between 1 and 7.
- Transparency is naturally supported by GIF pictures.

When exporting PNG assets, keep in mind:

- Selecting Transparency results in 32-bit PNG files.
- Selecting Smaller The file produces 8-bit PNG images.
- Leaving the above options unselected results in 24-bit PNG assets.

Dimensions: Indicate the width and height of the picture asset. Since the width and height are automatically correlated, adjusting one will also alter the other. If you want to adjust the canvas bounds of the exported asset, see Canvas Size.

Scaling: Selecting the size of the exported picture is a useful feature when exporting files at different resolutions. Scaling also affects the overall size of the image.

Resampling: Choose a resampling method that modifies the amount of image data when modifying the resolution or pixel dimensions of an image, usually at the resizing stage.

1. **Bilinear:** Provides medium-quality results by introducing pixels by averaging the color values of neighboring pixels.

2. **Bicubic:** A slower, more accurate technique that looks at the values of nearby pixels. Compared to Bilinear or Nearest Neighbor approaches, Bicubic generates smoother tonal gradations through complex computations.

3. **Bicubic Smoother:** Designed to produce smoother results, this smoother method is perfect for expanding photos using Bicubic interpolation.

4. **Bicubic Sharper**: This tool improves sharpness while decreasing picture size via bicubic interpolation. With this technique, a

resampled image keeps its detail. If certain regions seem too sharp, think about using Bicubic.

5. **Bicubic Automatic**: Based on the image, this feature chooses the best Bicubic sampling technique automatically.

6. **Nearest Neighbor**: An image's pixels are duplicated using this quick but imprecise technique. Suitable for images with non-anti-aliased borders, maintaining crisp edges and resulting in reduced files. However, while scaling or executing several operations, use caution regarding potential jagged consequences.

7. **Preserve Details:** Emphasizes the need to maintain sharpness and picture details while scaling.

Canvas Size: Set the width and height values that your object requires as the canvas size. The preview will be resized using the Export As dialog to center the picture inside these parameters. This function is beneficial in several scenarios such as:

- Exporting icons in different sizes that must be centered in 50x50 px boxes.
- Exporting banner pictures with sizes that deviate from the specifications.

The picture is cropped to the set width and height values if it is larger than the canvas size. On the other hand, if the canvas size is greater than the picture, the extra area is filled in using the information in the image. When a backdrop layer is present, the background fills with white; when none is there and the format parameters permit transparency, the background turns translucent. It fills with the last swatch in the color table while in index color mode. The settings return to the ones specified in Image Size when you click Reset.

Metadata: Select whether you want the exported assets to have metadata, such as contact details and copyright.

Color Space: Designate the following choices' default selections:

- Whether to change the exported asset's color space to sRGB.
- If the color profile should be included in the exported asset.

Export as Location Preference

To change the Export Choose your preferred location by using one of these techniques:

1. Select Export from the Edit > Preferences menu.

2. Choose Export Preferences under File > Export.

Select one of the following options under Export As Location in the Preferences dialog box:

- Export resources to the current document's location.
- Export assets to the final address provided.

Export Layers as files

Use these instructions to export and save layers as separate files with automated layer naming in a variety of formats, including PSD, BMP, JPEG, PDF, Targa, and TIFF.

1. Select File > Export > Export Layers to Files..

2. Choose the following options in the Export Layers To Files dialog box:

- Select the destination for the exported files by clicking Browse under Destination. The files are automatically stored in the same location as the original file.
- Type a name into the File Name field. To give the files a shared name, use the Prefix text box.

- In the Layers panel, select the Visible Layers Only option if you want to export just the layers that have visibility enabled. This is helpful if you wish to have specific layers removed from the export.
- Using the File Type menu, select a file type, then set up any other settings you require.
- If you would want to incorporate the working space profile into the exported file—which is necessary for color-managed workflows—you may optionally choose to Include ICC Profile.
- Select Run to start the export procedure.

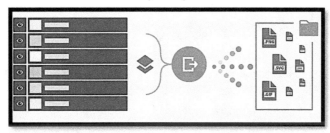

Export artboards as files

To export Photoshop artboards as separate files, take the following actions:

1. Select File > Export > Artboards to Files from the menu.
2. Carry out the subsequent operations in the Artboards To Files dialog:
   - Decide on a location to save the generated files.
   - Specify a file name prefix.
   - Specify whether overlapping regions should be included in the exported artboard content.
   - Choose if you want to export the artboard backgrounds in addition to the artboards.

- Decide whether to export artboard backgrounds along with the artboards.
- Select the appropriate export file format, such as PNG-8, PNG-24, JPEG, PDF, PSD, Targa, TIFF, or BMP.
- Configure the export settings for the selected file type.
- Indicate if you want the exported artboard names to be exported alongside the artboards. If you'd like, you may change the font's size, color, and canvas extension color.
- Select Run. The artboards will be exported by Photoshop as files in the chosen format.

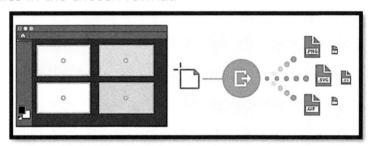

Export the artboard as PDFs.

To export Photoshop artboards as PDF documents, take the following actions:

1. Select File > Export > Artboards to PDF.
2. Carry out the subsequent operations in the Artboards To PDF dialog:
   - Select the location where the created PDF documents should be saved.
   - Give the PDF documents a file name prefix (e.g., Campaign insurance).
   - Select whether to export content that overlaps the artboards or just the stuff that is on the artboards.

- Indicate which artboards to export—all of them or just the ones you presently have selected.
- Select if you want to export the backgrounds from the artboards with the artboards.
- Choose whether to produce one PDF document per artboard or one PDF document for all of the artboards in the current document. When creating several PDFs, the prefix given for the file name is used in each one.
- Choose between ZIP and JPEG encoding for the produced PDF documents. Choose a Quality level (0–12) if you're using JPEG.
- Choose whether to export PDF documents with the International Color Consortium (ICC) Profile included. Color input or output devices are characterized by an ICC profile.
- Indicate if you want the names of the artboards to be exported alongside the artboards. If you'd like, you may change the font's size, color, and canvas extension color.
- Select Run. Photoshop will use the provided parameters to create the PDF document.

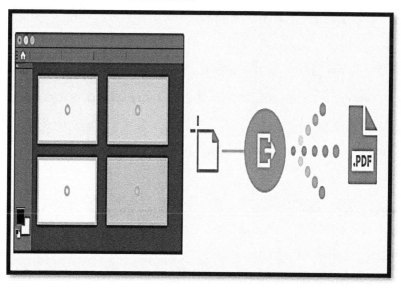

How to create a shared album and invite people to contribute (Lightroom Bonus)

Sharing and inviting people to see or participate in an album is now simple. You also can pick pictures that aren't in any albums yet, send them out by invitation, and ask people to contribute. Convenient access to all of your selected photographs in one place is ensured by this simplified method.

To share an album and extend an invitation to others, take these actions:

1. Navigate to the Albums section, select an album, or start from scratch. Alternately, use the Grid view to pick many photographs. After making your decision, choose one of the subsequent steps**:**

- On macOS, use the keyboard shortcut Ctrl-click, or on Windows, use the context menu to select "Share & Invite" after selecting the album or selected photographs.
- Select the "Share & Invite" icon located in the upper-right corner of the grid header.
- Select "Share & Invite" by clicking the ellipsis in the top-right corner. In case the album has already been shared, you have the option to select one of the individual icons located in the upper-right corner.

2. Select "Get shareable link" to get the album URL that you have shared.

3. The Link Access box has "Invite only" selected by default. This creates a private link, so the only people who can access or edit your album are the ones you invite.

As an alternative, you can make your album publicly accessible by changing the Link Access setting to "Anyone can view" and enabling anybody with the link to view it.

4. Select the symbol to duplicate the URL and distribute it. You may share the album on Facebook or Twitter by clicking their buttons, provided that your Link Access option is set to "Anyone can view."

In the "Invite" area, enter the email addresses of those you would like to invite to see or collaborate on your album, then click "Invite." An email with access to your album will be sent to the invitees.

5. The email addresses you've issued invites to may be viewed in the "Invite" section. Use the drop-down list next to each email address to set up the album access option for that individual:

- **Can View:** The invitee can view the shared album, add comments to photos, and mark them as Favorites.

- **Can Contribute:** The person who received the invitation can upload images to the shared album, provide comments on individual images, and favorite certain shots.

- **Can Edit and Contribute:** The invitee is authorized to modify and contribute images by adding them to the shared album. Many people can modify a single photo, and you can see the different adjustments in the Versions panel's Auto tab. Invitees can also export the pictures in JPG format.

- **Remove Access:** This option removes the invitee from the shared album list.

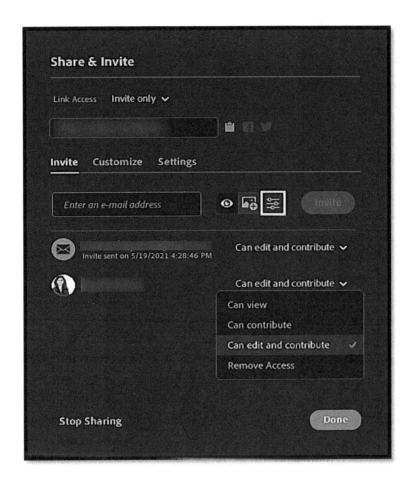

There is a record of people's access requests under the "Invite" section. Next to each request, click to grant or deny the person making the request access to the album.

6. Select the "Customize" option in the "Share & Invite" dialog box to examine and change the following settings:

- **Title:** Presents the name of the record. Choose not to reveal the name. The name of the current album is shown by default. The time and date that you created the link are shown as the title if you have chosen a group of images in the grid.

- **Author:** Provides the name of the individual who created the connection. To conceal the name, deselect.

- **Theme:** Select the layout of images you want to share from options including Photo Grid, One-Up, and Column.
- **Appearance:** Choose a dark or light color scheme for the photo layout.

Click "Customize on the web" to access further editing choices, where you can add text, rearrange photographs in your shared album, and do much more.

7. The "Settings" tab allows you to modify the following configurations:

Under General:

- **Allow JPG Downloads:** If you check this box, other people will be able to download the shared collection of pictures.

- **Show Metadata**: Turn this feature on so that people may see the metadata linked to the shared photo collection.

- **Show Location Data:** To grant people access to location data associated with the shared photo collection, activate the "Show Location Data" feature. To keep your location hidden, deselect it.

- **Allow Comments and Likes**: By default, this option is enabled, which enables visitors to your shared photographs to leave likes and comments. Choose not to like and comment on it if you want viewers to stay away.

Under Link:

- Allow Access Requests: Requests for permission to see your shared photographs can be made using the "Allow Access Requests" option, which is the default setting.

8. Hit "Done." The creation of your group album has been completed.

NB: Click the icon on the left side to modify the group album's sharing preferences. To see a list of shared albums, expand the Photos folder in the Shared to Web panel. From there, you have a choice between the following options:

1. Select the appropriate album by performing a right-click (Windows) or control-click (Mac) and selecting "Share & Invite" from the context menu.

2. Select the "Share & Invite" button, which is situated in the grid header's upper-right corner.

3. Click the ellipsis in the grid header's upper-right corner, then choose "Share & Invite.."

CHAPTER ELEVEN

TROUBLESHOOTING ISSUES

Known issues in Photoshop

This article lists all of the Photoshop bugs that have been found. Please report any issues you run into to the Photoshop community if they aren't covered here.

Compatibility with macOS:

- Ventura: macOS 13.0 is compatible with both Photoshop and Ventura.

- Monterey: macOS 12.0 is compatible with Photoshop and Monterey.

- Big Sur: macOS 11.0 is compatible with both Photoshop and Big Sur.

Apple Silicon Issues:

M1 Native Problems: For further information, see "Photoshop for Apple Silicon.

Problem with Rosetta Compatibility: Select Subject in Select and Mask may not be able to identify the subject in portrait photos while using Rosetta mode. We are working closely with Apple to identify and fix this problem.

Scratch Disk Full Errors:

Issue: 'Scratch disk full' errors usually mean that there is not enough storage space left on the hard drive or drives that have been assigned as scratch disks to complete a task.

Crash When Using the Remove Tool:

Issue: Encountering a crash when attempting to use the Remove tool in Photoshop.

Resolution:

1. Verify that the drivers for your GPU are current.

2. Choose the "More Stable" option from Preferences > Image Processing > Remove Tool Processing.

[Windows] Crash When Using Select Subject or Object Selection Tool:

Issue: Experiencing crashes when using the Object Selection tool, Select and Mask in Photoshop.

Resolution: Refer to the community thread for additional information and solutions. Update your Nvidia driver from the official website.

Please note that these recommendations aim to address the specified issues.

Unavailable Tools and Options:

Issue: The Adjustments panel with presets is missing, making it inaccessible in Photoshop.

Solution: We are aware of this issue and are actively working on resolving it.

In the meantime, as a workaround, relaunch Photoshop twice to view the new Adjustments panel with presets.

Interoperability Errors:

Issue: Difficulty in Integrating Lightroom Desktop Photos into Photoshop

- **Description:** Masks for JPEG, HEIC, TIFF, PNG, and PSD files imported from Lightroom desktop may need to be recomputed in Adobe Camera Raw for the adjustments to appear correctly. Sometimes the masks are not found in their original configuration.

- **Solution:**

- Export images to your local computer from Lightroom.
- Make use of Lightroom's export menu by choosing "Edit in Photoshop.."

Issue: Photoshop cannot be browsed in Bridge.

Description: Clicking File > does not start Bridge. Look through In Bridge from inside Photoshop.

Solution:
- Uninstall Bridge and Photoshop from your machine.
- Rename the following DB folders:
- C:\Program Files (x86)\Common Files\Adobe\Adobe PCD
- C:\Program Files (x86)\Common Files\Adobe\caps
- Reinstall both Bridge and Photoshop that you uninstalled in Step 1.
- Optionally, try switching to Bridge from Photoshop using the Alt+Tab keys. Note that this is not supported on Mac ARM.

Install application updates

1. On your PC, start the Creative Cloud desktop application.
2. Select Preferences by clicking on the Account symbol in the top right corner.
3. In the left sidebar, select "Apps" and enable Auto-update for all apps or specify the ones you want to update automatically.

4. Alternatively, you can manually update your apps by choosing "Updates" from the left sidebar or navigating to Apps > Manage updates from the right sidebar.

5. In the Updates screen, click on "Update" to update the desired app.

Install operating system updates

You can address numerous issues by ensuring your operating system is up-to-date.

For information about macOS, see Get software updates for your Mac. Adobe suggests testing on a non-production partition to confirm that new operating systems are compatible with your current hardware and drivers. For Windows, visit the "Windows Service Pack and Update Center.

Install graphics card (GPU) driver updates

Uncertain whether your graphics processor or driver is the source of your Photoshop issues. Disabling GPU acceleration will help you find the source of the problem.

Locate Performance under Edit > Preferences > Windows or Performance under Photoshop > Preferences > MacOS.

Proceed to uncheck "Use Graphics Processor."

Start Photoshop again.

Resolve GPU and Graphics Driver Issues

1. For Windows: Update your graphics driver

Updating your graphics driver can resolve various issues, including crashes, incorrectly rendered images and performance problems. Obtain driver updates directly from the video card manufacturer.

2. Verify Your Cache Levels Setting

Reset Cache Levels to the default setting of 4, which is 1. Select Edit > Preferences > Performance 2. Set Cache Levels to 4, 3. Quit and relaunch Photoshop 4. After restarting Photoshop, try the steps that caused the issue again. If you have Photoshop preferences set to 1, you may experience performance issues with features that utilize the graphics processor

3. Reset Your Preferences

The Graphics Processor settings return to their original state when preferences are reset. For further guidance, see "Restore preference files to default." Launch Photoshop after resetting your settings, then follow the actions that caused the problem again.

4. Adjust Your Advanced Settings for Open CL

a. Choose Edit > Preferences > Performance

b. In the Performance panel, click Advanced Settings

c. Disable Open CL

d. Quit and restart Photoshop for the change to take effect.

Update macOS

Apple regularly provides updates with bug fixes and integrates GPU drivers into the system software. Install any system updates or security patches that are available, then restart your Mac. If you are unable to install the most recent version of macOS on your computer, it may be a sign that your hardware does not support the current versions of the operating system and Photoshop. It could be required to utilize an earlier version in some situations.

of Photoshop that aligns with the release date of your current operating system version.

Keep Photoshop Updated

Photoshop has been updated to include all of the most recent bug fixes. The best reliable experience should come from utilizing the most recent version of Photoshop and macOS if your machine meets the current requirements.

Maintain Multiple Photoshop Versions

It is up to you to keep many copies of Photoshop on your computer as needed. The performance of other versions won't be impacted if one version is removed. Go to the Creative Cloud desktop program, select the uninstall option by clicking the three dots in the lower right corner of the application description credit card, and then delete the application.

Address Creative Cloud Issues

If you encounter crashes, especially when opening new files, the Creative Cloud application could be the potential source of the problem.

Disable the GPU

To troubleshoot, consider turning off the GPU in Photoshop preferences. Follow these steps:

1. Select Performance under Preferences in Photoshop.
2. Proceed to disable "Use Graphics Processor."
3. Restart Photoshop.

If the problems disappear with the GPU disabled, you can choose to work without it or explore additional steps below to address the issues.

Address Camera Raw Issues

Examine your preferences and settings within Camera Raw to ensure optimal performance and image quality. Consider making adjustments to various options such as cache size, color space, preview mode, and workflow settings.

Uninstall and then reinstall Photoshop. This action can address potential issues with corrupted files or settings that might be hindering the proper functioning of Camera Raw.

Turn off Automatic Graphics Switching

Go to Edit > Preferences > Performance (Windows) or Photoshop > Preferences > Performance (macOS). Ensure that "Use Graphics Processor" is chosen in the Graphics Processor Settings section within the Performance panel. Click the Advanced Settings button to access the Graphics Processor Settings dialog box. Unselect the "Enable Automatic Graphics Switching" option and click OK. Finally, restart Photoshop.

Troubleshoot Plug-ins

Ensure Your Plug-Ins Are Up to Date

The most recent version of your plug-ins may be found by visiting the manufacturer's website. Many times, plug-in-related problems may be fixed by downloading and installing the latest versions. For installation or reinstallation of their plug-ins, use the plug-in installer provided by the manufacturer.

Restore preferences

Resetting Photoshop's Preferences file goes beyond resetting preferences; it also affects color settings, custom keyboard shortcuts, and creating workspaces. Ensure you save these if you wish to retain them before proceeding with the reset.

Resetting Photoshop Preferences

Step 1: Select a preference from the menu field

- Select General from the Preferences menu by clicking the Edit menu on a Windows computer.
- Select General from the Preferences menu by clicking on the Photoshop menu on a Mac.

Step 2: Select "Reset Preferences on Quit"

- Look for the "Reset Preferences on Quit" option in the General Options section of the Preferences menu field. Choose it.

Step 3: Click "Yes" to erase the settings when you're done.

- When you close Photoshop, a little popup window will ask if you wish to reset the preferences. To confirm, click OK.

Step 4: Exit and Open Photoshop Again

- Close Photoshop by selecting File -> Exit in Windows or Photoshop -> Close Photoshop in Mac OS.
- Photoshop will start up with the default options when you restart it.

Troubleshoot fonts

If you're experiencing crashes in Photoshop, especially during startup or while working with Type, consider these three troubleshooting steps for font-related issues.

1. Reset Photoshop's Preferences

Resetting Photoshop's preferences involve backing up and restoring them, which will hide the Character panel and reset the selected tool to the default Move tool. For detailed instructions, refer to the guide on manually removing the Photoshop Settings folder.

Manually removing preference files is the most comprehensive method to restore Photoshop to its default state. This approach ensures that all preferences and user presets causing potential issues are not loaded.

Here are the steps to follow:

1. Quit Photoshop.
2. Navigate to Photoshop's Preferences folder.
   - Adobe Photoshop [version] is located in Users/ [user name]/Library/Preferences on macOS. Configurations.
   - Windows: Adobe/Adobe Photoshop [version]/Adobe Photoshop [version]/Users/[user name]/AppData/Roaming\ Configurations.

Note: The user Library folder is hidden by default on macOS. To access files in the hidden user Library folder.

3. Drag the entire "Adobe Photoshop [Version] Settings" folder to the desktop or another safe location for a backup of your settings.
4. Launch Photoshop.

Automatically, new preference files will be generated in their original place.

2. Reset Photoshop's Font Cache

Resetting the Photoshop font cache allows the software to generate a new enumerated font list.

The Photoshop font cache contains the enumerated list of installed fonts and font features that Photoshop utilizes. Deleting this cache file allows Photoshop to generate a new one.

MacOS:

1. Close the desktop version of Creative Cloud and Photoshop.
2. Open Adobe Photoshop by going to /Users/[user name]/Library/Application Support/Adobe.
3. Empty the Trash and remove the "CT Font Cache" folder.

WINDOWS:

1. Close the Creative Cloud desktop application and Photoshop.
2. Open Adobe Photoshop <version> from \Users[user name]\AppData\Roaming\Adobe\Adobe.
3. Empty the Recycle Bin and remove the "CT Font Cache" folder.

Restart Photoshop and Turn off Font Preview

After restarting Photoshop, navigate to Type > Font Preview Size and select none. This action turns off Font Preview, preventing Photoshop from rendering previews for any potentially damaged installed fonts.

Photoshop is crashing

Resetting your Photoshop settings is one of the first things you should do when you have a problem with Photoshop. Take these actions:

1. Press and hold Alt+Control+Shift (Windows) or Option+Command+Shift (macOS) immediately after launching Photoshop.
2. A request to remove the current settings will appear.

Alternatively, if Photoshop is already running, you can reset preferences upon quitting by navigating to General Preferences > General > Reset on Quit.

Missing Tools

To reset the toolbar, take these actions:

1. Select Toolbar > Edit..

2. Click "Restore Defaults."

3. Click "Done.

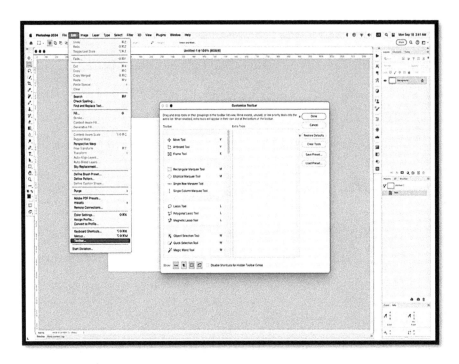

Start with safe-made

At times, third-party extensions and utilities may disrupt Photoshop's functionality. Starting your computer in safe mode can help troubleshoot and resolve the issue by disabling these third-party elements.

MacOS:

- Starting up in safe mode: On macOS, safe mode disables all third-party extensions and startup items, running only essential kernel extensions and Apple-installed startup items.

Windows:

- Start your computer in safe mode: On Windows, safe mode initiates Windows with a restricted set of files and drivers.

Troubleshoot update errors

Many of Photoshop's update issues might be caused by corrupted or missing program files. Tools for cleaning up your disk, such as MacKeeper or CleanMyMac, may be part of the problem. Make sure your cleanup tools are updated frequently to handle this or think about not using them at all.

INDEX

Drawing Tools, 25

197, 200, 201, 204, 208, 210,
218, 220, 225, 227, 228, 231,
233, 234, 237, 243, 245, 247,
249, 250, 251, 254, 255, 257,
258, 269, 276, 277, 278, 280,
281, 282, 288, 290, 291, 293,
294, 295

Pixel art, 125

plug-ins, 310

preset brush, 239, 240, 241

R

RAW files, 121

Remove tool, 283, 284, 285,
286, 305

retouching, 2, 15, 22, 99

Retouching Tools, 21

rotate text, 266

S

Selection Tools, 15

Slice and Crop, 16

snapshot, 39, 83, 181, 182, 183,
184, 186, 187, 188, 217

software, 1, 2, 4, 5, 36, 40, 75,
83, 87, 88, 96, 167, 307, 308,
313

Spot Healing Brush, 22, 279

Start menu, 9

Status Bar, 32, 33

T

Tool presets, 67, 239, 245

Tool Properties panel, 29, 30

toolbar, 10, 14, 26, 27, 35, 61,
110, 114, 126, 130, 131, 134,
151, 152, 153, 154, 155, 168,
172, 174, 175, 181, 188, 191,
192, 214, 215, 216, 253, 260,
262, 270, 271, 274, 279, 288,
314

type Tools, 19

V

Variable font, 165

Vibrance, 199, 200, 201

W

Windows, 2, 4, 5, 9, 10, 29, 37,
54, 57, 58, 70, 71, 89, 90, 91,
92, 100, 106, 121, 122, 125,
130, 134, 136, 138, 139, 140,
167, 168, 170, 171, 172, 180,
185, 187, 190, 192, 196, 203,
205, 209, 210, 217, 233, 241,
242, 249, 251, 253, 258, 261,
264, 271, 273, 275, 277, 282,
284, 288, 289, 290, 300, 303,
305, 307, 310, 311, 312, 313,
314, 315

Z